*How to
Cope with
the Developing
Financial Crisis*

ASHBY BLADEN

How to Cope with the Developing Financial Crisis

McGRAW-HILL BOOK COMPANY
New York St. Louis San Francisco Auckland Bogotá
Düsseldorf Johannesburg London Madrid
Mexico Montreal New Delhi Panama
Paris São Paulo Singapore
Sydney Tokyo Toronto

Library of Congress Cataloging in Publication Data

Bladen, Ashby
    How to cope with the developing financial crisis.

    Includes index.
    1. Debts, Public—United States.   2. Finance—
United States.   3. International finance.   I. Title.
HJ8119.B57   336.73   79-13272
ISBN 0-07-005547-5

1234567890   BPBP   89876543210

*In this book, the masculine pronoun "he" has occasionally been used to
refer to both sexes for the sake of simplicity.*

*The editor for this book was Kiril Sokoloff,
the designer was Naomi Auerbach, and the
production supervisor was Sally Fliess.
It was set in Palatino by University Graphics.*

Printed and bound by The Book Press.

Dedication

*Since this book will have some harsh things to say
about academic economists in general, it is appropriate
to begin by noting some of the exceptions. You will find
references to some of the academics who understand
how the financial system works scattered throughout;
but I owe an especial debt of gratitude to Professor
Charles Kindleberger, and to Professors Martin
Feldstein and Peter Gutmann.*

*There is also a group of economically sophisticated
men who are deeply involved with the financial
markets, several of whom are becoming increasingly
outspoken about the damage that political forces are
inflicting upon our financial system. I have learned
much from all of them, and I am proud to call most of
them my friends. They are all grand gentlemen, and I
choose to list them by the names by which they are
familiarly known to financial market participants in
spite of the fact that three of them are Directors, and
one is Chairman, of my Company. George Conklin, Roy
Reierson, Jim O'Leary, Fred Simmons, Sidney Homer,
Al Sommers, Henry Kaufman, Sam Nakagama, Al
Wojnilower, and Gary Shilling; to these gentlemen this
book is respectfully and affectionately dedicated.*

Contents

vii

Preface

A Reform of Financial Theory Is Needed in Order to Make the Current Inflationary Chaos Understandable

The coming crash in house prices

The inflationary overexpansion of debt, both within the United States and several other countries as well as internationally, has reached a level from which a soft landing into price and financial stability is no longer feasible. A painful crash is inevitable sooner or later, and the longer we try to put it off by doing additional inflationary things the more painful it will be when it does happen. In the United States we have already had a series of crashes in specific markets that hurt primarily business people and investors, but the next one will most probably hurt the majority of American families because it is virtually certain to involve the prices of houses. A long series of unwise political policies has produced a bubble in house prices that cannot be sustained indefinitely even though its popping is likely to cause a substantial downturn in consumer spending, and therefore a serious recession.

The amount of debt outstanding is a crucially import economic variable

The fundamental cause of each of the localized crashes that have already occurred, and of the crash in house prices that looms ahead, is the excessive rate of debt formation that has been going on at an accelerating pace for many years. The main reason why its painful consequences were not generally recognized in time to prevent it from producing an unsustainable inflation of house prices is that ever since the Keynesian revolution in Economics that occurred during the late 1930's academic economists have foisted upon us some theories about the financial system that are remarkably contrary to the facts as they are perceived by practical financial managers. These current theories suggest that neither the rate of debt formation nor the total amount of debt outstanding is an important economic variable. This view, which contradicts both common sense and practical experience, has made it impossible for most economists to understand, let alone predict, the steadily worsening disorders that have plagued the American financial system since 1965 and the international financial system since 1970.

The disastrous consequences of the post-1936 economists' miscomprehension of the way that our financial system really works are developing so rapidly now that the time has come to attempt to rescue financial theory from the grasp of the academics. Practical people do not usually concern themselves with the reform of theory unless they have found that the existing theory leads to unsatisfactory results in the real world. In recent years the unsatisfactory practical results of much conventional economic analysis have become increasingly obvious; and by now a revolution in Economics, led to a considerable extent by people who are not themselves professional economists, is developing. This book is an attempt to initiate a reform of financial theory as my contribution to the broader revolution.

Why a reform of financial theory is important to you

There are three reasons why all Americans, not just economists and financial types, should be interested in the improvement of financial theory. First, it seems clear that unless there is a fundamental change in our national policies the United States is headed for a British-style inflationary disaster. However, the road to inflationary disaster also contains a number of deflationary potholes in specific markets. We have already bounced through several of them, and we are about to fall into the biggest one yet in the housing market. You will be better able to foresee the potholes ahead and take the necessary financial steps, which are the exact opposite of the policies that work best most of the time during an inflation, if you understand the process by which the potholes are formed.

Financial turmoil is inevitable until at least 1981

Second, it does not appear to be politically feasible to get off the road to disaster before 1981 at the earliest; and thereafter the long-run prospects for this country will depend upon whether we are wise enough to elect in 1980 politicians to both the Congress and the White House who are determined to get off the inflationary road at any cost because they understand that its ultimate destination is disaster. The American economy already shows all the statistical symptoms of the British disease. However, while Britain has suffered from it for many years and by now has probably been too weakened to recover fully, we have caught it only recently; and we can get well again if we can muster the political courage to take the necessary medicine. But if we fail to seize the opportunity to get off the road to inflationary disaster that is provided by the national elections of 1980, we can get a good idea of what our economy and society will look like by the time we get another such opportunity by taking a glance at contemporary Britain.

Financial troubles can cause
a social disaster

Finally, I will argue that anything beyond a quite modest degree of social democracy, rather less than we now have in the United States and considerably less than they have in Britain, cannot be provided in real terms because the level of taxation that would be required would constitute a crushing disincentive to the productive efforts upon which the national standard of living depends. The attempt to provide an excessive degree of social democracy in nominal terms by the inflationary overexpansion of debt has already substantially eroded the real value of the savings that the American people hold in the form of financial claims; and if this process continues after 1981 it is perfectly capable of causing a social disaster that, in the United States at least, would very likely be accompanied by considerable civil disorder and violence. I find it necessary to speak out about these unpleasant things that most of us would rather not think about because financial managers like myself, and the productive and responsible people whose savings we are paid to look after, are becoming endangered species. If we do not get off the road to disaster after 1980, productive people who have accumulated some savings are going to have to rethink their life-styles, the places in which they live and their plans for retirement as well as the ways in which they earn their livings and the forms in which they hold their savings.

I hope that much of what I have to say, particularly about the reform of financial theory, will prove to be of lasting significance; but many of the specific forecasts and recommendations that you will find in this book are necessarily topical. The publishers have been most cooperative about rushing it into print as quickly as possible; but events are moving very rapidly now, and many things have already happened that bear upon the argument. Specifically, the revolution in Iran and the subsequent intensification of the oil crisis, the accident at Three Mile Island, and the national elections in Canada and the United Kingdom are all extremely relevant; but since their ultimate consequences are not yet foreseeable I have made no attempt to bring the rest of the book up to date. Three Mile Island does not alter the fundamental points that I made about the electric utility industry in Chapter 9; but it may produce another crisis, and another investment opportunity of the type described in that chapter. It is also beginning to look as though Iran will turn out to be the "last straw" that is discussed in the final chapter.

One development that does seem to call for further comment is the growing awareness of the fact that the American standard of living is declining. With the announcement of the April consumer price index both Chairman Kahn and Director Bosworth of the Council on Wage and Price Stability told us that we must expect a period of real austerity and a decline in our standard of living. However, they did not elaborate upon the fact that their own efforts have contributed significantly to that decline.

One of the main points of this book is that we cannot expect to go on indefinitely maintaining a higher standard of living than we are earning through our own productive efforts by borrowing enormous sums from foreigners and selling off our productive assets in order to pay for imported oil. Sooner or later we will simply have to adjust to the world market price for petroleum, and that will indeed involve a moderate fall in our national standard of living. Beyond that inevitable adjustment however, instead of passively accepting a declining standard of living I believe that it is far better, and much more in keeping with the spirit that originally created the American standard of living, to restore the conditions in which we, as individuals, will again have an adequate incentive to roll up our sleeves and go to work to produce a high standard of living. You will find an analysis of the reasons why we are ceasing to do that in Chapter 6, and an account of the steps that must be taken if we are to go back to doing it in Chapter 8.

Ashby Bladen
June 4, 1979

Economics from a Financial Point of View

The purposes of this book

This book has four main purposes. The first is to demonstrate that the intensifying financial disorders that we have suffered since 1965 are *not* merely unrelated incidents—just a case of one damned thing going wrong after another—but are rather the natural consequences of a pair of interrelated systematic processes, one domestic and the other international. Since these processes *are* systematic, they are analyzable and their consequences are foreseeable—not with absolute precision, but accurately enough to provide a basis for practical business and investment decisions. In order to document this point, the appendix contains the forecast that I prepared at the beginning of 1969, on the basis of which the pension funds that I was then managing came through the severe bear market of the following eighteen months virtually unscathed.

The second purpose is to attempt to lessen the almost exclusive emphasis that modern Economics places upon mathematics and to restore some of the attention that used to be given to psychological factors. Specifically, I will argue that changes in the burden of debts upon incomes affect the real economy largely through their impact upon the degree of confidence with which borrowers and lenders view their future prospects. I know that economists have been trying for many years to get rid of the concept of confidence because it is inherently qualitative and its employment compromises the attempt to make Economics into an exact quantitative science; but I believe that what is lost in theoretical precision will be more than made up for in practical effectiveness. At least, I have found that to be so in my work as an investment manager.

A number of the financial economists who are involved with interpreting and forecasting the investment markets have suggested that what is presently called monetary policy should be conducted in the light of the rate of expansion or contraction of the total amount of debt outstanding rather than of one or several of the monetary aggregates. I agree; but so far none of them has told us *why* the overall rate of credit expansion is the most relevant factor. Thus, the third purpose of this book is to explain just how I believe our financial system really works, why it is currently producing an excessive rate of debt formation, and what the consequences will be if it is not stopped.

The last purpose is to appeal to the common sense and instinct for self-preservation of the American people in order to urge them to demand financial common sense of our political leaders. I will attempt to analyze clearly the enormous differences both in principle and in practical results between prudent finance, as it is carried on by many financial institutions, and political finance as it is exemplified by such programs as the Social Security system; and I will point out that the inflationary consequences of the latter can largely negate the efforts of responsible people to provide for their own future needs and responsibilities by means of the former.

In the international sphere, both we and the people of much of the rest of the world have already suffered greatly from the consequences of the increasing irresponsibility that American financial policy has demonstrated during most of the last two decades; and yet I cannot conceive of any feasible substitute for, or successor to, the United States in the role of the non-communist world's financial leader. Other countries, especially the strong currency countries, will undoubtedly play a larger part in the world financial system from now on; but if we cannot or will not function as the leader nobody else will be able to either, and the financial world will begin to fall apart again as it did after 1931 when Great Britain ceased to be able to act as the world's financial leader. Following the reasoning of Professor Charles P. Kindleberger's invaluable book *The World in Depression 1929– 39,*[1] I will argue that it was largely the consequences of that event that caused the slump of 1930 to develop into the Great Depression.

The enormous loans that have been made to politically shaky and economically weak countries, particularly since the oil price explosion in late 1973, should be a topic for discussion in this book because they are one of the main sources of the rapidly increasing fragility of the world's financial system. However I will cover them only in the most general terms, partly because a detailed analysis would be unmanageable in a relatively brief book and partly because it is impossible to predict just how that bubble will pop. The international financial system had become similarly fragile by the beginning of the 1930's, and the general consensus is that the financial difficulties of the Credit-Anstalt, a bank located in the politically weak and economically absurd Republic of Austria, precipitated the final collapse that culminated in the American bank holiday of 1933.[2]

**A major cause of the soaring burden
of debts worldwide is the fact that the
financial limits to transfer payments
are being exceeded**

As a specific example of the kinds of policy changes that are required, this book will attempt to find a practical answer to

[1]University of California Press, 1973.
[2]For a particularly clear and concise account of the Credit-Anstalt affair see *The World in Depression*, pp. 148–151.

the dispute between nineteenth century liberalism which maintains that the general welfare is best served if people are encouraged to produce as much as their energies and intelligence will allow by being permitted to keep as much of the fruits of their own labors as possible, and twentieth century social democratic liberalism, which maintains first that people are entitled to economic benefits as a matter of right, and second that the individual shares of those benefits should be as nearly equal as possible. This practical solution will be achieved by defining the limits within which equalizing incomes through transfer payments is feasible.

The matter is urgent because the current uneasy compromise between these two versions of liberalism is visibly breaking down. At the moment, both in the United States and a great many other countries, we are still attempting to run the productive side of the economy according to the nineteenth century liberal principle of rewards in proportion to contributions while we are simulteneously moving steadily in the direction of more equal benefits, without reference to productive contributions, by using taxes and transfer payments to redistribute incomes. This venture is in rapidly increasing danger of foundering upon the rock of financial inviability because in most countries today the political authorities are attempting to redistribute a greater amount of economic benefits from the more to the less productive members of their societies than the productive sector is willing to pay in taxes; and this attempt has two obvious consequences.

The resulting inflation causes social discord

First, since it is not politically feasible to levy sufficient taxes upon the productive sector to provide the benefits promised to the unproductive sector, virtually all social democracies are running large and rapidly increasing national budget deficits. Thus nominal purchasing power is being created by Government borrowing at a rate in excess of that at which real goods and services available to be purchased are being produced, and the inevitable result is an accelerating rate of inflation. Inflation constitutes, in effect, an additional but hidden tax upon the productive sector levied through the declining real purchasing power of its nominal income; and therefore twentieth century liberals often tend to think that a little inflation is a good thing. However, inflation also reduces the real value of the promises that have been made to the relatively or completely unproductive members of the society; and as this effect becomes increasingly obvious with the acceleration of inflation, they quite naturally feel that they are being cheated. Inflation is a great provoker of social resentment and discord; and by now social discord has become a serious problem in several social democratic countries, notably including the United States.

And the taxes cause tax evasion

A second consequence of rising taxes and growing political interference in the economy is that they create an increasing incentive to drop out of the visible economy and join what has aptly been called the subterranean economy where you can charge whatever the market will bear, and ignore the tax collector altogether by dealing only in cash and keeping no accessible records. The size of the subterranean economy is not easily determinable; but in the United States it is obviously large, and growing rapidly. The bigger it becomes the less visible income remains for the tax collector to levy upon; and at some point our American system of self-assessment of income taxes will clearly break down. These conditions indicate that there are inherent limits to the amount of social democracy that can be imposed upon the productive economy without adverse financial consequences; and that by now many countries have seriously exceeded those limits.

The audiences to whom this book is addressed

This book is addressed primarily to the concerned layman who senses that something is going badly wrong in our economy and financial system, and realizes that he is not being given an adequate explanation of just what it is that is going wrong. Much of the book is concerned with the rather technical problem of reforming financial theory, but I have attempted throughout to state just what the problem is and the nature of the solutions that I am objecting to as well as my own proposals in the hope that readers who have not had any specific education in Economics will find the argument reasonably easy to follow. Some of it will be very familiar to readers who have had such an education, but I hope that the attempt to view these matters from the perspective of a financier[3] rather than from that of an academic economist will keep this trip over ground that has already been well traveled from becoming a bore. I am afraid that professional economists will scorn this effort because it contains no algebra whatsoever,[4] but it may give them a useful insight into the way that practical investment decision-makers look at things.

I am also afraid that contemporary liberals of the social democratic variety will find this book distasteful. It is perhaps an unfortunate fact, but it is a fact nevertheless, that most people (and countries) are more willing to allow part of their wealth to be transferred to other people (and countries) at a time when they are optimistic about their own prospects than they are when they are skeptical about the likelihood that they will become wealthier themselves. By now we have imposed upon the productive sector of our economy a burden of taxes to finance transfer payments (including foreign aid) and all the other costs of modern government that many

[3]I know that the word "financier" has pejorative connotations in common speech, but I believe it to be a useful word nevertheless. If "finance" is the correct word for the activities of raising and investing funds, what else would we call a person who engages in those activities? Incidentally, I prefer to use the words "finance" and "financial" to refer only to those activities, not to the bookkeeping, budgeting and reviewing activities that are the functions of the controller and the auditor. The fact that in some organizations the same person performs all of these activities has caused an unfortunate semantical confusion.

[4]Well, there is one equation; but it is not my fault. It is a traditional one that I maintain is no longer relevant to today's circumstances.

people will not willingly pay—with the consequences that the incentive to work hard to earn another pretax dollar is shrinking, the incidence of tax evasion is increasing, and optimism is becoming a scarce commodity in America.

Why social democrats should take heed

The issue here is basically the one about the size of the pie versus the size of the slices; but it is unreasonable for people who are concerned that everyone should have a satisfactory slice not to be concerned about the total size of the pie. The burdens that political decisions have imposed upon the productive sector of our economy are steadily widening the gap between the pie that we do have and the pie that we could have; and this trend bodes ill for the continuation of liberal policies with respect to the distribution of the slices either within this country or between the nations. The amount of productive efforts that people are willing to make varies to a considerable extent according to the amount of the wealth they have produced that they are allowed to keep; and at some level, well short of the level that we have reached in the United States, the burden of taxes becomes counterproductive.

A subtler point, but one more directly germane to the main argument of this book, is that substituting the hidden tax of inflation that results from excessive debt formation, both upon the part of government and of businesses and people reacting to inflationary governmental policies, for some of the burden of open and aboveboard taxation has all of the short-run consequences of taxation (*except* that one that counts most with politicians—the onus of having voted for the taxes) combined with longer-run consequences that can range from serious to catastrophic.

The nature of financial disaster

Most modern social democracies are already experiencing serious difficulties as a result of inflation, but it may not yet be clear to you that we are headed in the direction of disaster. The blunt fact is that the logical end-result of the irresponsible national financial policies that we have been following since the early 1960's would be a total collapse of our present financial system, which provides for people's future needs and responsibilities by issuing intangible financial claims to goods and services that will be produced in the future, in exchange for currently existing resources that will facilitate the production of those future goods and services. I will demonstrate that such a financial system contributes enormously to human welfare, but also that its continued existence depends upon human attitudes and habits that were extremely rewarding during the last century but that make no logical sense today. At present we are coasting on the momentum of habits that social democracy and inflation appear to have rendered obsolete, and the momentum is clearly beginning to run down. One of the most ominous factors in the domestic situation is that since 1975 the American people have begun to adjust their habits to the inflationary environment by borrowing more and saving less than had been their custom; and I will explore some of the implications of that change in Chapters 6 and 7.

If the rate of debt formation in the United States does not moderate very soon it is likely to produce a serious intensification of domestic inflation because the private sector will tend to stop saving altogether, with the consequence that the only way that real productive investments can be financed will be by Federal Government debt formation that commands real resources through the hidden tax of inflation. Internationally it is likely to lead to an indefinitely prolonged fall in the external value of the dollar that will in turn cause a progressive reduction of world trade as Americans become less and less able to afford imports, and the governments of countries whose people save and invest much more than we now do attempt to protect their workers and industries from a flood of American exports that have become extremely cheap in terms of their own currencies. That will also reverse the rising trend in the standard of living that has occurred since World War II in most countries that have been able to maintain civil order, and if the reversal goes far enough it could produce another Great Depression. In these circumstances the willingness as well as the ability to provide transfer payments, either domestically or internationally, would be severely impaired. These are the things that the American people should be thinking about as the 1980 election approaches.

Responsible financial managers should take the lead in persuading the American people that a fundamental change in policy is essential if we are to avoid disaster

The last chapter is the only one that deals specifically with questions of investment management, but wherever it is relevant I have attempted to illustrate the interplay between sound theory and profitable practice by examples drawn from my professional work as an investment decision-maker. Moreover, the main thesis of the book has obvious implications for investment policy that other investment managers may wish to ponder. To put that thesis into a nutshell, it is that the financial system is simply a network of human institutions and practices that can break down and disappear if it is abused badly enough; and that accelerating inflation and a soaring burden of debts are clear indications that it is indeed being seriously abused. Therefore, the final audience to whom this book is addressed consists of the responsible officers and employees of financial institutions who are accustomed to taking the long view and to pondering the ultimate consequences of their actions.

It is axiomatic that the "long run" for politicians extends through the next election; but we in the life insurance industry, for example, frequently have to consider what the results of today's decisions may be twenty, fifty and even a hundred years in the future. I will argue that continuing to find politically expedient short-term solutions to the steadily worsening financial difficulties that past political expedients have created risks an eventual collapse of the financial system as a whole, which would have catastrophic consequences for all of humanity. There is still time to prevent such a calamity, and indeed I sense that the tide of public opinion has already turned away from expediency toward responsibility; but the reform will proceed most smoothly and effectively if it is led by the people who best understand the ways in which our financial system works in practice, and the human and social conditions upon which its satisfactory functioning depend. The pains and frustrations that a return to financial reality must inevitably cause will be borne without social discord and strife only to the extent that the general public becomes aware that the course we are presently embarked upon leads ultimately to disaster so that a change of direction is absolutely essential.

The key to this book

I began to develop the point of view expressed in these pages in 1961, in the course of attempting to determine what the financial consequences of the New Economics of the Kennedy Administration would be. Since we know as a matter of empirical fact that during good times debts grow a great deal faster than incomes, it seemed to me that the proposal to run the economy permanently at full employment implied that the burden of debt service charges - that is, interest payments and principal repayments - would also have to rise faster than incomes forever. And that, of course, is in the end a mathematical impossibility.

That insight is the source of and the key to almost everything that is to be found herein. What it amounts to is simply the macroeconomic application of the concept of the coverage of debt service charges by income that is a basic principle of the practical microeconomic art of credit analysis. I can hardly claim that it is a stroke of intellectual genius; but the implications for economic policy appear to me to be enormous. When they are fully developed, they amount to a theory of the financial system that is considerably at variance with both the Keynesian and the monetarist approaches, which between them constitute the generally accepted conventional wisdom on the subject. The acid test that suggests that this is the more valid and useful approach is that it indicates clearly that an excessive rate of debt formation will, if it goes on long enough, produce first accelerating inflation and then steadily intensifying financial disorders; while the other two approaches tend either to deny or to obscure those consequences. In this respect, the record of the last dozen years speaks for itself.

Thus the present form of this theory, which is presented in Chapters 2 through 7, is the result of many years of pondering these matters; but by 1962 the major implications had become sufficiently clear to me that when I left the Connecticut Mutual Life Insurance Company in February of that year I went to its President and suggested that he consider the possibility that accelerating inflation might produce an upsurge in interest rates to a level high enough to cause substantial withdrawals of funds from life insurance companies through policy loans and surrenders, at a time when low market prices for bonds would make raising the funds a painful process. Now, at that time inflation was nonexistent, interest rates and bond prices were stable, and withdrawals of funds from life insurance companies had not been a problem for thirty years. The then-President of Connecticut Mutual is far too kind a gentleman to let it show, but I am sure that he concluded that I was simply an eccentric whose departure from his organization was probably a good thing. However when I next ran into him, shortly after the great increase in policy loans during 1969 and 1970, he was gracious enough to recall the incident and to say that perhaps he should have taken it more seriously.

What you will find in this book

Chapter 1 begins the necessary destructive task of clearing the financial field of obsolete and mistaken theories by attacking the approaches and attitudes of post-1936 economists in general terms. Any reader who has been fortunate enough not to have been exposed to economic doctrines since that year need not concern himself with the criticism of unsound approaches, but should plunge in with Chapter 2. Chapters 2, 3, and 4 attempt to explain how the financial system does work in practice. Chapter 5 tells what it accomplishes when it is working well, and Chapter 6 tells why it has been working progressively less well in recent years. Chapter 7 covers the prerequisite conditions for the existence of an international financial system capable of financing world prosperity and progress, and the appalling irresponsibility of American external policy that destroyed those conditions. Chapter 8 makes some suggestions about national financial policy, and Chapter 9 discusses the significance of all this for you, the reader.

ONE

The Trouble with Economists

The complete victory of mathematical over literary economics has been too complete for its own good

Before 1936 there existed two kinds of economists. There was the fascinated observer of human affairs in all their diversity and complexity, the first and perhaps still the greatest of whom to be recognized as specifically an economist was Adam Smith. And then there was the abstract reasoner, who attempted to demonstrate that all the blooming, buzzing confusion of the marketplace really illustrated certain logical and universal principles that could best be expressed in terms of algebraic equations. The first, and arguably still the greatest of these, at least in the sense that he laid the foundations upon which everyone who has come after has built, was David Ricardo. Both the Smiths and the Ricardos were attempting to make logical sense of the human activities and institutions that are involved with the creation, preservation and distribution of wealth; but for the Smiths the primary emphasis rests upon the facts to be explained while for the Ricardos the primary emphasis is upon the explanatory principles. Any reader who is familiar with nineteenth century American Philosophy will find it helpful if I refer to the Smiths as pragmatists and the Ricardos as transcendentalists. The rest will not find it helpful, and I hope that they will ignore the preceding sentence.

Until 1936 there was a reasonable number of both Smiths and Ricardos, both were recognized as economists; and indeed it was not considered disreputable for a professional economist both to engage in detailed analysis and description of human activities and institutions and to reason abstractly or mathematically about the general principles that they illustrate. However, since 1936 all that has changed; and today only the Ricardos retain the full status of professional economists. People who concentrate overmuch on the practical details of human affairs are dubbed journalists, empiricists or, at best, "literary economists."

The proximate cause of this change in attitude is perfectly clear. J. M. Keynes' *General Theory of Employment Interest and Money*, published in 1936, was an intellectual tour de force that demonstrated that all changes in the level of total incomes and output can be explained as the consequences of changes in the balance between the general public's propensity to save and the business community's propensity to invest, in the context of a series of algebraic equations that determine precisely what offsetting change in Government policy is necessary to produce the optimum level of output.

Note that there is no *logical* incompatibility between Keynes' demonstration, that a mathematically adequate explanation of all changes in output and incomes as consequences of changes in the propensities to save and to invest is always available, and psychological explanations of the same phenomena in terms of changes in the state of confidence. However, there is a psychological incompatibility. Most professional economists who have taken their degrees since 1936 are by nature, and all of them are by academic training, essentially mathematicians; and like all good mathematicians they have a professional prejudice in favor of the most simple and elegant solution to any problem and against any logically unnecessary details or complications. Mathematicians and logicians are taught to respect the principle known as Occam's razor, according to which everything that is not logically required to demonstrate a conclusion should be shaved away. Therefore, since Keynes had demonstrated that all changes in output and incomes can be explained as the result of changes in the propensities to invest and to consume, any further details or speculations are unnecessary and redundant.

This intellectual prejudice that has been inculcated in all professional economists of recent vintage is a great stumbling block to communication between them and practical people, particularly market participants, who know very well that psychological conditions are so important in the marketplace that sensitivity to them or the lack thereof often makes the difference between making a bundle and losing your shirt. Even today, when the professional economists who earn their living by advising market participants are beginning to turn their attention to the study of panics and crashes for the first time in forty years, Professor Charles Kindleberger (who narrowly escaped indoctrination by finishing his class work in Economics in June 1936 and whose professional virtue one would have thought to be beyond question by now) found it necessary to defend his conduct in publishing a book with the title *Manias, Panics and Crashes*[1] against the criticism that real economists should rise above the study of such exciting and seductive but thoroughly unprofessional matters. Since I have frequently cited Professor Alvin Hansen as being largely responsible for the almost universal tendency among American academics to oversimplify and make a doctrine out of Keynes' in fact remarkably broad-gauged writings, I am grateful to Professor Kindleberger's new book for reminding us that Hansen specifically argued that Keynes had rendered the older psychological theories of economic fluctuations obsolete. The practical result of this prejudice is that most self-respecting economists have ignored what used

[1]Basic Books, Inc., New York, 1978.

to be called "the state of credit" for more than forty years, with the consequence that on the rare but important occasions when the state of credit becomes a crucial variable their predictive and policy-prescribing models go wildly awry. Since this has been happening with increasing frequency in recent years, and with increasingly disastrous results, I conclude that a reformation of the theory is very much in order.

The obsession with recession

One rather odd consequence of the post-Keynesian refusal to recognize that the rate of debt formation is a relevant factor is that throughout the powerful and sustained economic expansion of 1975–1979 we were constantly bombarded from all sides by predictions of imminent recession. In effect, the prophets of recession were forecasting what the responses of people, businesses and some governmental bodies would be to the very high level of debts outstanding and the record levels to which many interest rates had risen, in advance of the actual occurrence of those responses.

However I will point out, in Chapter 6, that the *effective* rate of interest that determines whether people desire to borrow or not is the difference between the stated rate of interest and the expected rate of inflation; and that did not appear to be high at all. One can make an extremely good case for the view that as long as people are more worried about what inflation is doing to the real value of their incomes and savings than they are about the amount of debt that they have incurred they will continue to borrow and spend so that both the expansion and the inflation will continue. If that is so, then when people do slow down on the borrowing and spending because they have become more worried about the level of their debts than about inflation, the resulting downturn is unlikely to be mild. My own view at the time was that the next decline in economic activity would be caused by financial difficulties, not merely high nominal interest rates;

and that it would come much later and be a good deal more severe than was generally expected. The chief reason for this prolonged obsession with recession was the fact that almost everyone sensed that something was seriously wrong in our economy; but since it is now impermissible to worry about financial conditions the only things left that current economic theory allows you to worry about are changes in the level of real output.

The American economy is not a closed system

Another obvious but by now catastrophic mistake that the American disciples of Keynes made stems from the fact that he wrote the *General Theory* as a theory of a closed system— that is, an economy that does not participate in international trade or financial flows. Being an Englishman, Keynes was not so stupid as to believe that a closed economy actually exists. For him it was a simplifying assumption that permitted him to concentrate on the points he wanted to make about national economic policy without going into all the complications that recognizing the world environment would involve. Unfortunately, the academics who popularized his doctrines in this country believed that the American economy came close enough to being self-sufficient that it could usefully be treated as a closed system; and from that day to this Economics has been taught in the United States primarily as the theory of a closed system. If the course runs on schedule, the Professor will devote the last couple of classes to international trade and finance. If it lags, he omits them and considers that no harm is done. During the 1960's, when I was arguing that our persistent balance of payments deficit was undermining our role as the non-communist world's political and financial leader, many people who considered themselves to be economically literate simply could not see that this was a problem, with the result that it has now become a disaster.

How stable is the real world?

The key question at issue between the mathematical and the literary economists is whether all the important economic relationships are so stable that the economy can be adequately described in a series of invariant algebraic equations. If they are, then once the economists have got the equations just right and fed them into the computer they can all go off on sabbatical and leave the computer to handle the practically important but intellectually rather uninteresting job of issuing economic forecasts and policy prescriptions. On the other hand, if fundamental relationships are apt to change from time to time then a model consisting of invariant equations will, no matter how perfectly it was originally synchronized with the real world, eventually get out of kilter; and the literary economist's fascination with what real people are actually doing and thinking is required to ferret out whatever it is that has changed so that the mathematical economist can readjust the model appropriately. Since 1975, for example, the models have consistently underestimated spending for consumption and overestimated personal saving by projecting their historical relationships to personal incomes; while in the real world the rising tide of social democracy and inflation has caused the American people to reduce the amount of their incomes that they save substantially, and perhaps permanently.

Theory should reflect what real people actually do

That is the theoretical problem. In fact, however, the practical difficulties are more serious and occur more frequently than does the occasional need to adjust the model for fundamental changes in the real world. An almost universal characteristic of the pure mathematical economist that practical people find extremely galling is his lack of serious interest— perhaps disdain is not too strong a word— for what is actually going on out there in the real world. His chief interest—often his passion—is for building mathematical models. Any superficially plausible theoretical description of reality that affords a basis for specifying the equations is good enough for him; and as I mentioned earlier the simpler and more elegant the theoretical description is the better he likes it even though the real world is frequently neither simple nor elegant. (The great power of modern computers makes it easy for mathematical economists to operate extremely complex models involving hundreds of variables, but that is another matter. I am talking about the effort, or lack of it, that is invested in the task of determining how well the underlying theoretical description upon which the model is based corresponds to the reality that it is supposed to describe; and the preference of mathematical economists for simple descriptions of complex phenomena is notorious.) The consequence is that the practical experts in most fields usually consider that the theoretical description of their area of expertise misses most of the important points.

The efficient market hypothesis

In my own business (investments), for example, we have a very simple and elegant description of the relevant human behavior. The efficient market hypothesis asserts that investors know all that there is to be known about any particular security and its issuer, and that they are cold-bloodedly rational about making investment decisions. Therefore, the market price of a security is necessarily the correct price at the moment because it reflects the sum total of rational judgments based upon all the knowable facts. And since the current price is the correct one, the investment of much effort and intelligence in the attempt to outperform the market is unrewarding. The best that the investor can hope for is to do approximately as well as the market. Mathematical economists have tested this conclusion six ways to Sunday, and indeed they have demonstrated conclusively that very few investors do consistently outperform the market. Nevertheless, most competent professional investors would agree that the underlying hypothesis is ridiculous because practical experience has taught us that we almost never know everything that is relevant to a given decision, and we most certainly do not always act rationally. Indeed one very competent investment professional, David Dreman, wrote a book[2] that demonstrates that most investors fail to do well precisely because they do not usually employ rational analysis— indeed, they normally do not think for themselves at all but simply follow the herd. That is something that you cannot afford to do, as we shall see in the last chapter.

Investment analysis cannot be completely quantified

Academic economists are always trying to devise mathematical models that will enable investment managers to be replaced by computers, and about once a decade I attend a seminar given by the International Business Machines Corporation to see how this enterprise is progressing. Invariably I conclude that they haven't got the key variables right. Let me give a reasonably simple example. One of the first such attempts involved quantifying the crucial concept of risk by relating it to the past price fluctuations of the security under review. I do not know any practical investment analyst who believes that that is the right way to go about it, and I suspect that risk is in the end unquantifiable so that investment analysis is likely always to contain a considerable element of art and is unlikely to evolve into a mathematical science. If academics would just spend some time in the investment departments of financial institutions finding out how practical investment decisions are actually made they might begin to get somewhere. But they are most unlikely to do that, and I always leave the IBM school in Poughkeepsie with the comfortable feeling that my job is safe for another decade.

The academics will undoubtedly protest that this criticism is most unfair, that in the course of building mathematical

---

[2]*Psychology and the Stock Market*, Amacon, New York, 1977.

models they frequently conduct exhaustive surveys to determine the attitudes and beliefs of the business community. It is true that every professor who has access to a computer believes that he has an inalienable right to bombard the business world with multiple-choice questionnaires, but having been the recipient of many such I believe that I can put my finger on the difficulty. The questionnaires are often designed from the point of view of a preconceived theory or as a means of testing alternative hypotheses, none of which may strike the practical expert as being the most useful way of looking at the matter. If an economist undertaking the investigation of a particular area of human activity would just sit down and ask the practitioners questions like What are the most important problems? What do you do about them? What are the measures of success or failure? he would gain some real insight even though he would not be able to score the results with a computer. It is not necessary to become a technical expert in all aspects of the matter (even Adam Smith, in the most famous of such investigations, characterized the soldering of the head on a pin as "a curious business"), but it is highly desirable to find out what the practical experts consider the relevant factors to be.

Nor can the theory of credit

Credit is a particularly inappropriate candidate for mathematical treatment because it is inherently qualitative. The word itself derives from the past participle of the Latin verb credere—to believe, to trust; and the granting of credit is necessarily an act of faith indicating that the lender believes that the borrower will prove trustworthy. In order to remain creditworthy a borrower must act in a manner that tends to maintain his creditors' trust in him. That is a fact that most successful businesspeople seem to understand but that many economists and politicans obviously do not understand; and in recent years there have been numerous examples of governmental credits being severely damaged by irresponsible political actions. Several particularly striking and momentous examples of that process will be given in the course of this book. Other things being equal, I would rather make loans to prospering businesses than to governments because the moral risk appears to be less; and when they do go off the track the leverage that I can apply to get them back on it is usually much greater.

In Chapter 7 we will take a look at the ways in which the irresponsibility of the United States' external financial policy has damaged the creditworthiness of this country, which ever since World War II has been acting as a banker to the rest of the world, severely enough to suggest that an international financial crisis similar to the one that occurred in 1931–1933 is approaching. That irresponsibility has been perfectly obvious for nearly twenty years, but the vast majority of academic economists were too wrapped up in the minutia of internal policy to be aware of the fact that our external policies were very probably creating the conditions for another worldwide financial collapse.

TWO

How Purchasing Power Is Created

Purchasing power is created either by earning or by borrowing

One consequence of the failure of academic economists to consider what practical people actually think and do has been the creation of a great deal of intellectual confusion about a question that is, when considered from the right point of view, a fairly simple and straightforward matter. Everyone agrees that inflation is caused by creating purchasing power at a more rapid rate than the supply of real goods and services available to be purchased is growing, but just how that is accomplished is not entirely clear. Before we plunge into the convolutions of academic theory, let us consider the matter from a practical point of view.

By far the most common way in which people get purchasing power is to earn it by doing something useful. This way of creating purchasing power has no impact upon the general price level because the value of the goods and services produced is equal to the value of the incomes that the production of those goods and services creates. At the most primitive level this identity of output and income is obvious. If

Robinson Crusoe has spent the day making a clay pot, then his income for the day is one clay pot. In more complex economies the identity is less obvious because most of us find that we can maximize our incomes by specializing in whatever it is that we do best and trading the particular fruits of our own labors for all the variety of things that we need and desire. To the extent that markets are free and competition is perfect, the rival bids and offers of buyers and sellers ensure that every particular person's income tends to equal the value of his productive contributions. Of course, markets are never completely free any more than competition is perfect,[1] so it is entirely possible that some people are underpaid or overpaid. Nevertheless one person's loss presumably is another person's gain; and in any case the economic statistician resolves the issue in the aggregate by defining the national income as identical to the national output. Therefore, in accordance with a definition that is reasonably well supported by common sense, the creation of purchasing power through the production of an equivalent amount of real goods and services that are available to be purchased cannot have any effect on the *general* price level. *Particular* prices will fluctuate as relative tastes and supplies vary from time to time, but there is no reason for the overall price level to change.

[1]One of the sophomoric arguments that radical economists often indulge in is to say that the market system does not work because it is not a perfect example of pure competition as the classical economists defined it. What human institution ever was perfect? The market system of organizing human efforts will never appeal to youthful idealism because it takes people as it finds them, does not assume that they can be perfected, and does not presume to kill or otherwise mistreat millions of existing, imperfect human beings for the sake of an ideal of future perfection. It does appeal to mature people who realize that it is simply the most productive form of organization that mankind has ever developed or is likely to develop, and that that is good enough for practical purposes. Pure competition is an abstract ideal just as pure communism is; but the practical system that it inspires results in a high standard of living and freedom of individual choice within a fairly broad range, while that which communism inspires results in tyranny and an economy that may be efficient at producing what the politicians want but that pays little attention to what individual human beings want.

There are some ways of obtaining real goods that do not involve current incomes and output. For example, nature provides us with a variety of goods free of charge. It is also possible to consume accumulated wealth. We are doing that in some sectors today, as witness the appalling state of many of the American railroads and also many of the older American cities. Letting physical assets deteriorate is at best a form of borrowing from the future when they will have to be put right, and at worst an invitation to disaster: eating the seed corn involves a dangerous reduction in the wealth of the community that threatens a famine next year. However, by definition consuming accumulated wealth does not create purchasing power.

A particular person can also gain purchasing power by gift or theft; but here again, one person's gain is another's loss and the identity between income and output is not affected. However, after earning an income by doing something useful the next most common way in which people get purchasing power is by borrowing it; and this is where the confusion begins. I do not believe that I have ever run across an explanation of the interrelationships between money, credit and purchasing power that does not strike me now, after I have had to think the matter through for myself, as being a complete muddle. Let us try to explore this intellectual briar patch by starting with the simple and moving progressively toward the complex.

A commercial code is fundamental to the existence of a financial system

I will start by elaborating a bit on some comments that Sidney Homer made in the first chapter of his monumental *History of Interest Rates*.[2] In informal societies the distinctions between earned income, gift, theft, loan and repayment may

---

[2] Second edition, Rutgers University Press, Brunswick, N.J., 1977. A marvelous book, highly recommended to anyone who wants to know more about the evolution of the financial system.

not be at all clear. Sidney Homer's example was a necktie in a fraternity house, and that is as good as any. When I discover that my roommate has beaten me to the tie that I had planned to wear tonight my immediate reaction is likely to be that he has stolen it, but he may well think otherwise. He may argue that he has simply borrowed it, or that neckties are fungible,[3] and that he is merely exacting the return of equal value for the tie that I liberated from him last weekend. However, over time humanity has found that the uncertainties and inefficiencies caused by the informality of such arrangements greatly impede important activities like getting to the party before the beer runs out; and so we have introduced clear definitions and established practices that members of the society are expected to abide by. In a fraternity house the code may be no more complicated than that Thou shalt not scrounge thy roommate's last necktie; but in the business world the rules are quite precise and detailed, and infractions result in penalties ranging from ostracism to imprisonment.

The financial system deals with loans and financial instruments

In this paragraph I will attempt to provide technical definitions of two key concepts, the implications of which will be explored in the next two chapters. A *loan* can be described in general terms as a transaction in which the borrower receives something now in exchange for a promise to return either that thing or something else (which may or may not be fungible with the thing lent) that is usually, but not necessarily, of more or less equivalent value to the thing borrowed; and a rent, called *interest*, may be charged for the use of the thing

---

[3]"Fungible" is the quality that market participants ascribe to things that are taken to be equivalent to each other even though they are not physically identical. If, for example, one stockbroker owes a hundred shares of General Motors common stock to another broker he does not have to return the specific certificate that he had borrowed, but is considered to have discharged his debt whenever he returns any certificate for one hundred shares of G.M.

borrowed.[4] If the values involved are significant, the promise to repay is usually put into writing; and it may be made a matter of public knowledge by procedures ranging from the traditional placing of a "tombstone" advertisement in the financial section of a newspaper to the formal recording of a mortgage with the County Registrar. If it were not for the existence of these written promises to repay our economic life would be a great deal simpler, but also far less convenient and productive—and I would not have had to write this book. I will define these written promises to pay, which can range in sophistication from the fraternity brother's I.O.U. or the gambler's mark on the one hand to the hundred page indenture and note of a private placement bond issue on the other, as *financial instruments*.

Financial instruments and purchasing power

What is the impact of credit transactions upon purchasing power? The most intuitively obvious answer is that the borrower has gained purchasing power from the lender, who in turn has given it up until the borrower repays it; and in an economy that lacks financial instruments and institutions that would clearly be the case. Just as I cannot wear the tie that my roommate has made off with, you cannot spend the hundred gold sovereigns that I have borrowed from you until I return them.

However, the evolution of a structured financial system, consisting of financial instruments and financial institutions that operate according to a recognized code that defines acceptable financial behavior, opens up other possibilities. *One* of those possibilities is recognized in current financial

---

[4]For the sake of formal completeness let me mention that occasionally a loan is made (or refinanced) by an arrangement according to which the borrower does not promise to repay the principal but instead undertakes to pay interest forever. Such an arrangement is properly called a *perpetual annuity*. The outstanding examples are the British Consolidated War Loans, or "Consols."

theory, but others are not in spite of the fact that they happen thousands of times every business day. Anyone who has taken a course in Economics or Money and Banking will find the following paragraphs familiar to the point of boredom; but I would like to walk you through the generally accepted theory of the way in which some financial transactions create purchasing power in order to demonstrate later that there exist other transactions that are closely analogous in practice, but that are *not* generally considered to create purchasing power.

The conventional theory of bank credit

Banking existed as a practical business for hundreds of years before it occurred to anybody that the extension of bank credit increases total purchasing power, but today it is generally accepted that that is the case. The demonstration proceeds more or less in the following manner: when you deposit a hundred dollars to your checking account with a commercial bank you continue to regard it as readily available purchasing power that is under your control because all you have to do to spend it is to write a check to a third party. If the bank then proceeds to lend your hundred dollars to someone else by depositing it in his checking account in exchange for his note, he has clearly gained purchasing power because now all he has to do to spend it is also simply to write a check. When he buys something with that hundred dollars he loses the purchasing power but the seller gains it; and while all this is going on you retain the right to withdraw your original hundred dollar deposit and spend it any time you please. Thus it appears that the act of making a bank loan causes the total amount of purchasing power to increase by the amount of the loan.

Let us consider briefly how this apparently paradoxical practice developed. As we shall see in Chapter 3, banks originally evolved out of the warehousing service that goldsmiths provided for people who held purchasing power in the form of bullion or coins made out of precious metals. Although the people who left their hoard of precious metals with the goldsmiths (and who will henceforth be referred to as *depositors*) always had the right to withdraw their deposits, the goldsmiths found that in practice large amounts remained with them for years on end so that it seemed reasonably prudent to earn an interest income by loaning a portion of them to third parties. Of course, whenever you lend out other people's property there is always a risk that an unexpected event will cause many or even all of the depositors to attempt to withdraw their deposits before you can get the borrowers to repay, thereby precipitating what has come to be called a banking crisis or panic; and we will review briefly the steps that have been taken over the years to insulate the financial system from such crises. Nevertheless, a goldsmith or banker who did not seek too greedily to maximize his income, but instead exercised a reasonable degree of prudence with respect to the portion of his deposits that he lent out, could expect to withstand all but the greatest shocks caused by unforeseen calamities.

The people who borrowed coins or bullion from the goldsmith obviously gained purchasing power, but the depositors did not consider that they had lost it because they relied upon the goldsmith to return their deposits whenever they wanted them. As a practical matter, since precious metals are heavy and awkward to carry around, merchants and tradesmen got into the habit of accepting the warehouse receipts that were issued as evidences of deposits by reputable goldsmiths as constituting satisfactory instruments for settling transactions; and loans were frequently made in the form of these receipts rather than in the underlying metals that backed them up. During the course of time the modern instruments of checks, bankbooks and bank notes evolved out of these warehouse receipts for precious metals.

As long as financial instruments remained closely linked to precious metals, inflation in the modern sense of the word was impossible because a fall in the purchasing power of financial instruments would simply cause people to exchange them for the underlying metals. The severing of the relatonship between financial instruments and precious metals, and the resulting onset of inflation, will be the subject of the next chapter. Let us accept for the moment the fact that the financial system now deals mainly in pieces of paper that in some as yet undetermined way represent purchasing power, and go on to consider whether it is true that the extension of bank credit expands purchasing power but that loans made by other financial institutions do not.

The safety and stability of bank credit expansion depend upon the existence of a financial system

If we look at just one bank in isolation, it is not entirely clear that the extension of bank credit expands purchasing power, or at least it would seem that it would be exceedingly risky to try to do this on any significant scale. A bank cannot loan out anything that has not previously been deposited in it. Also, a bank cannot pay off deposits that have been loaned out without calling in the loans, thereby extinguishing the purchasing power that the borrowers have received, except by realizing on the loans in some other manner. As long as people have confidence in the bank there is no reason why its deposits should shrink on balance. For every depositor who withdraws his deposit and uses it to buy something there will normally be a seller who deposits the proceeds of the sale in his bank account. But if the people understand that the bank cannot pay off any substantial part of its deposits without going through the time-consuming and risky process of calling a corresponding amount of its loans, they are very likely to become frightened and want their deposits back very badly because they themselves, or their friends or relatives, are also the debtors who will suddenly be squeezed by the calling in of the loans. Thus the idea that it is reasonably safe to create purchasing power by extending bank loans implies that there must be some reasonably reliable means by which banks can realize upon their loans without having to call them in. In fact, there are two ways of doing that. A bank can either sell its loans or use them as security for a loan to itself. The safety and solvency of the individual bank depends upon the existence of a financial system that is capable of providing new loans, and that also provides a market for existing financial instruments.

The financial system is underwritten
by the Sovereign State

Let us go one step further and consider an extreme situation. Suppose some disaster such as a plague develops and a very large number of people want to withdraw their deposits, in order to convert their wealth into forms that will be usable as purchasing power in remote areas where the financial system is rudimentary or nonexistent, so that the demands exceed the capacity of the banking system as a whole: what then? Major banking crises have happened from time to time—the last one in the United States occurred during the winter of 1932–1933—and the impact upon both the financial system and the real productive economy tended to be so severe that the political decision has been made to use the power of the National State to ensure, as far as seemed feasible, that it would not happen again. As we shall see in the next chapter, the Government of a National State can, as long as it retains effective control of the State, create all the purchasing power it wants by declaring its notes (or those of its creature, the Central Bank) to be legal tender and forcing the people to accept them. It can also lend those notes to a bank upon the security of its loan portfolio, or use them to buy financial instruments either from a particular bank or from the market as a whole. Thus it is generally recognized that the ultimate liquidity of the banking system is underwritten by the power of the State.

One of the most important points that I hope to make in this book is that if you look at the way that financial business is carried on in practice it becomes clear that other kinds of financial institutions are very similar to commercial banks in these respects and that, therefore, almost any credit transaction may in fact create purchasing power. The failure of economic theory to recognize this is a specific consequence of the academic economists' lack of interest in what practical men actually do from day to day.

We have seen that the fact that it is reasonably safe for banks to expand purchasing power by making loans depends first upon the existence of a financial system that is able to make additional loans to the banks, and to buy financial assets from them, and second upon the ability of the State to do the same things on an enormous scale if that appears to be necessary or advisable. The notion that other financial institutions do not create purchasing power implies that the same facilities are not open to them so that their loans are sunk investments, in the sense that when they make a loan they alienate the purchasing power until the loan is repaid. This further implies that their creditors cannot recapture the purchasing power that they have deposited with the nonbank institutions any faster than the loans mature and are paid off. I believe it is demonstrable that all of these implications are contrary to fact; and I will attempt to demonstrate it by using the example of the life insurance industry, partly because life insurance companies are generally considered to have the longest-term and least liquid assets and liabilities that are to be found in the financial system, and partly because I am personally most familiar with them.

If it were true that life insurance companies cannot realize upon our loans until they are paid off we would most likely be on the verge of real trouble right now. We are not generally considered to have liquid liabilities, but in fact the liquid liabilities of the industry total something over $150 billion. Roughly 90 percent of the reserves supporting our ordinary life policies are withdrawable either by surrendering the policy in exchange for its cash value or by taking out a policy loan, which is a matter of contractual right, and at a contractually set interest rate that is currently less than half the interest rate that just about any other kind of a loan would bear today.[5] Some of our other liabilities are highly liquid too, and as the inflation worsens it is probable that the withdrawals from life insurance companies will soar.[6]

Speaking as a practicing investment officer of a life insurance company, I do *not* consider that our existing assets are sunk investments. Every morning I try to appraise the relative merits of all the financial instruments that are legally available to us, and if I see something that I like better than something that we already own I can and do *sell* the less attractive investment in order to buy the more attractive one. Or, if the circumstances suggest that it is an appropriate thing to do, I can and do *borrow*[7] temporarily from the banks in order to make the new investment without first having to decide just which investment I want to liquidate. Normally these borrowings are modest by comparison with the total financial assets of the Company; and since the acceleration of inflation suggests that we may be hit with a major increase in policy loans we currently not only have no borrowings outstanding and a fairly large amount of liquid short-term investments, but we have also arranged much larger lines of credit than usual so that we can withstand a severe drain without having to cease making investments or perhaps even having to sell bonds in what is already a period of extremely high interest rates and therefore of low prices for bonds.

[5]Most of the borrowable cash values belong to policies that were issued years ago, when the policy loan interest rate was typically 5 percent. In the late 1970's, after endemic inflation and high nominal interest rates had become serious problems, the legally permitted interest rate was raised to 8 percent; and most new policies stipulate that rate. I regard this reform as technically defective: since there is no telling how high nominal rates of interest may go in an endemic and accelerating inflation, the policy loan interest rate should be a floating one that is tied to the rate that we can get on alternative investments. The notion of an interest rate that is fixed for the life of the insurance policy contract is one example of the many anachronisms in our financial system that were introduced during the nineteenth century when prices and long-term interest rates were far more stable than they are today. As we shall see in Chapter 6, these anachronisms are capable of creating serious problems in our current highly volatile and unstable markets.

[6]A forecast of the first really serious upsurge of policy loans that I wrote at the beginning of 1969, on the basis of the line of reasoning that is being developed in this book, is reprinted in the appendix in order to demonstrate that these things are foreseeable with sufficient accuracy for practical business purposes. A specific example of the interplay between sound theory and remunerative practice is that it was probably my sending of this forecast to the Chief Investment Officer of the Guardian Life Insurance Company that led him to hire me as his successor when he became President two years later.

[7]Technically speaking, we do not borrow but instead enter into a "warehouse agreement" whereby the bank purchases the investment subject to our commitment to buy it from them at a time that is convenient to us. The practical effect is much the same as a 100 percent collateral loan.

Conventional theory overlooks the secondary market for investment assets

It seems clear that the notion that an increase in the amount of bank credit outstanding expands purchasing power but that the expansion of other forms of credit does not is another example of the failure of academic economists to pay sufficient attention to the day to day activities of the practical business and financial world. In the real world, if a financial institution has not received additional deposits, but it wants to make some new loans nevertheless, it simply sells on the secondary market some of the financial instruments that it already holds, or posts them as collateral for a loan from another financial institution. Those are exactly the same things that a commercial bank does. Banks are unique in some respects, particularly in their role as lenders of last resort to the rest of the financial system, but they are not at all unique in their ability to create purchasing power.

The fact that *one* financial institution can make additional loans by selling or pledging its existing ones does not necessarily prove that the financial system as a whole can do the same thing. If total deposits are not rising, would not the financial institution that is buying or rediscounting loans, from the one that is raising new funds, also have to sell or rediscount a corresponding amount of its own holdings so that the total assets and liabilities of the financial system as a whole would not change? The answer is that that would necessarily be the case *if total deposits did not rise,* but in fact it would be most unusual for the resources of the financial system not to increase sufficiently to meet the total demands that are being made upon it.

To see why this is so, let us return first to the consideration of an extreme situation. In Chapter 4 I will describe the ways in which accelerating inflation, which is created by the excessive use of credit, in turn produces first a further excessive demand for credit and soaring interest rates and then an increasing tendency for financial crises to break out. Suppose that at some time in the future (and quite possibly not very far in the future) a further acceleration of inflation produces a huge demand for policy loans that exceeds the combined abilities of the life insurance companies and their banks to provide, what would happen? We have seen that in the extreme case of a run on the banks the Government would and has mobilized the credit of the State, which is in principle unlimited, to provide the necessary liquidity to prevent a financial collapse. Economic theory recognizes this fact, but it is silent about what would happen in the case of a run on the life insurance companies.

The answer is that exactly the same thing would happen. The risk that a suspension of payments by a large life insurance company would touch off a major panic is too great for the Government to be able to stand idly by. In the particular context of the American financial system the regional Federal Reserve Bank would make reserves available to the hardpressed life insurance company's commercial bank with the understanding that it in turn make funds available to take care of the problem. A major run on policy loans would also force life insurance companies to sell bonds in sufficient quantities to cause the bond market to collapse, and the Government cannot afford to let that happen either. In the American system, the Fed would buy financial instruments from the market in sufficient quantities to offset the selling by the life insurance companies, thus supporting the bond market at some viable level. Once again, the cases of the commercial banks and the life insurance companies are closely analogous. In extremis, the credit of the National State would be mobilized to underwrite the liquidity of both industries, and of any other major part of the financial system that got into trouble through no particular fault of its own.

This process does not function merely in extreme situations: in practical fact it goes on nearly all the time. For at least the last half century in most countries, and for a lot longer than that in some, the State has undertaken the responsiblity for seeing to it that credit is readily available, and at a reasonable cost, practically all of the time. It does this by mobilizing its own credit, usually through the intermediation of the Central Bank, to assure that financial assets, and therefore the financial system as a whole, remain satisfactorily liquid. In recent years there has also been a growing tendency for the State to lend its own credit to finance specific projects that the politicians believe to be more important or desirable than the financial market considers them to be. Just how this works, and its consequences both for good and for bad, are the main subjects of this book.

Given the great depth and liquidity of the American financial system, it is difficult to specify just what we mean by creating purchasing power. One aspect of the developing revolution in Economics is that we are beginning to realize that we were so traumatized by the experience of the Great Depression that we have tended to believe that the key problem is the creation of sufficient purchasing power to keep the economy from slumping, when in fact the worst problem in recent years has been that our ability to produce real goods and services has lagged so badly behind our ability to create purchasing power that it has caused a serious and accelerating inflation.

A reasonable answer is that purchasing power has been created whenever some party in the economy becomes more likely to buy something but no other party becomes less likely to do so. That happens when somebody earns more income by increasing his production of real goods and services; and it also happens when one party gains purchasing power by issuing a financial instrument in exchange for it, and the holder of that instrument believes that he can easily turn it back into available purchasing power by selling it or borrowing against it. For example, in my professional work as an investment manager, the chance that I will make an investment today is not significantly affected by whether or not I made one yesterday; it is affected almost exclusively by the attractiveness of the investments I am offered today relative to the ones that my Company already owns. Thus, in the end the question whether purchasing power was created by a financial transaction is determined by the lender's opinion about the liquidity of the financial instrument that he has received. We will return to the question of liquidity in the next chapter.

THREE

Just What Is It That Gets Borrowed and Lent? The Natural History of Money and Credit

The intuitively obvious answer to the question of what it is that gets borrowed and lent is, of course, money. That *seems* obvious because we are in the habit of measuring and recording financial transactions in terms of monetary units; but after pondering the matter for much of the last two decades I find that answer so ambiguous as to be virtually meaningless. It also has implications about the ways in which our financial system works and can be controlled that I believe to be incorrect.

Money with intrinsic value

Let us start by taking a look at the evolution of money. In primitive societies whatever real good proves easiest to transport, store and exchange gets used in ways that we would regard as monetary transactions. Livestock and grains have frequently been so used, as well as precious stones and metals. In time, however, gold and silver in the form of bullion or coins guaranteed to be of standard weight and fineness by the Sovereign or the State proved to be so much the most convenient kinds of money that they became nearly universal.

Note that the kinds of money that we have talked about so far consist of real things and can be considered to be commodities as well as money, so that when the stock of money that possesses tangible value increases the stock of real goods also necessarily increases by the same amount. A large increase in the production of gold or silver might cause the prices of other goods and services to rise relative to coins and bullion, but a more accurate way of describing the situation would be to say that the increasing availability of precious metals was causing their prices to fall. Attempts were certainly made from time to time to create purchasing power out of thin air—that is, without also working to produce an equivalent amount of real goods and services. It was done by clipping or alloying the coins, but that was an entirely different and enormously less efficient process than the modern inflationary abuse of the financial system. So let's move on to credit money.

Credit money

The next major step in the evolution of our present financial system resulted from the fact that, although coins and bullion were the most convenient forms of money with tangible value, they still left a good deal to be desired. Large amounts of them were heavy, and their value made it necessary to keep them in a safe place. Most people didn't have safe places, but goldsmiths by the very nature of their business did. So people fell into the habit of leaving their gold with the local goldsmith in exchange for a paper receipt. Then merchants in the neighborhood who knew and trusted the goldsmith adopted the habit of accepting his receipts in exchange for real goods and services; thus turning them into a paper money that did not possess, but that was backed by, tangible value. And finally, as the system evolved the goldsmiths realized that, since little if any of the gold ever left their vaults while their receipts were accepted as representing real purchasing power, they could earn an interest income either by lending out some of the gold or by issuing additional receipts in exchange for a note of the borrower instead of gold. That was the origin of the modern system of fractional-reserve banking—a system that until fairly recently was still based upon tangible value but in which the tangible assets of the financial system were no longer sufficient to pay off all of its liabilities. From that time on the financial instruments that were accepted as embodying purchasing power were based more and more upon credit—that is, on faith in somebody's future ability and willingness to repay—and less and less upon intrinsic value.

Constructive versus inflationary uses of credit

As long as the credit thus created was extended only to responsible people who had an opportunity to invest it in the tools and machines that make human efforts more productive all was well, for the resulting increase in real output enabled borrowers not only to repay the purchasing power that had been lent to them but also to pay a reasonable rent for its use. The fundamental cause of the accelerating inflation and worsening financial difficulties that we are enduring today is the fact that more and more of the credit that is being created at a rapidly rising rate is going to finance consumption, and incomes for people who do not produce a corresponding amount of real goods or services, and less and less is going to finance real investment in productive assets. Thus nominal demand is growing at an increasingly more rapid clip than is the supply of real goods and services.

Modern politics—the art of promising the ultimately impossible

The chief offender in this respect is the political system. In modern social democracies politics has become an art not of the possible, but of making promises of economic and social benefits that are often completely divorced from any responsible consideration of the practical possibility of fulfilling them in real terms. The attempt to appear to fulfill them, by creating nominal incomes at a rate substantially faster than that at which real output and real incomes are growing, is causing the great majority of national governments to run large and secularly increasing budget deficits that in turn produce rates of inflation, and consequently levels of interest rates, with which the financial system, as it is presently constituted, cannot in the end coexist. The substitution of Government financing for the present financial system, which is based upon personal savings—a process that is already well under way in most countries—is also virtually certain to continue to produce both accelerating inflation and a decline in the rate at which the productivity of the real economy is advancing. If it goes far enough, it can cause an actual decline in productivity.

Next to war, this is the most serious problem facing modern society. Faltering productivity, accelerating inflation and soaring interest rates have already caused steadily worsening economic and financial troubles; and they are capable of producing a disaster if their causes are not identified more accurately than they generally have been to date, and prompt steps are not taken to correct them. This book is an attempt to contribute to the improved understanding of our financial system that is urgently required if we are to reverse the current trend toward disaster. Perhaps it will turn out to be an elegy. The philosopher Hegel used to say that the owl of Minerva flies at dusk, and it may be the case that we will achieve an accurate understanding of the way our financial system works only as it is passing from the scene.

Early forms of credit money—
bubbles, assignats and continental dollars

In addition to the deposit receipts that we have already discussed, there is another and more disreputable forerunner of our modern financial instruments. During times of war monarchs and national states often mobilized the resources of their people by offering them in exchange notes of the State that were to be paid off at some time after the war was over. Often force and fraud were more characteristic of these loans than was confidence in the borrower. When Ethan Allen asks you to patriotically sell your horse to the revolutionary forces, proffering a fistful of Continental dollars in one hand and a horse pistol in the other, you are not likely to keep him waiting too long while you ponder the odds that after the war the Continental Congress will be able to make good on its wartime debts. The Continental dollars were supposed to be redeemed eventually with Spanish silver dollars,[1] which in the eighteenth century were the most common and universally accepted examples of money with intrinsic value; but of course neither the Continental Congress nor the individual states had any significant amount of silver dollars, or any plausible way of getting them. During the declining years of absolute monarchy in the seventeenth century this type of finance was common in France and Spain and, to a somewhat lesser extent, in Britain under the Stuarts; and, of course, it was revived in the eighteenth century by the revolutionary governments in the United States and France.

The consequences of forcing people to hold their savings in the form of claims against the Government whose real value was doubtful ranged from bad to disastrous. In Spain the national credit was virtually destroyed, and it has not yet entirely recovered. In France the chaotic state of the national

---

[1]Language often preserves the memory of things that have long disappeared from the scene. Coin was scarce in the American colonies, but the Spanish milled dollars made up a good part of what there was. They were worth 8 reales each in the Spanish monetary system, and in order to make change the colonists frequently split them into eight parts. Hence the piratical "pieces of eight," and the slang expressions "two bits" and "four bits" for quarters and half-dollars, respectively. I will point out later that the penumbra of connotations of ancient and long-vanished things that surrounds the word "money" still makes it psychologically difficult for us to bring our theoretical description of the financial system into conformity with the way that it actually functions today.

finances at the beginning of the eighteenth century enabled a remarkable Scottish financial adventurer, John Law, to attempt to pay off the national debt by exchanging it for shares of the original concept stock, that of the Mississippi Company which had been granted a monopoly on trading with the colony of Louisiana. As long as the stock went up so that people who had taken it in exchange for their claims against the Government showed a large profit the scheme worked; but in 1720 some sailors who had actually been to Louisiana returned to Paris and spread the word that it was not Golconda but a pestilential swamp. The resulting crash, followed three quarters of a century later by revolution, hyperinflation and the collapse of the financial system, left the French with an abiding mistrust of financial instruments and institutions; and the resulting limited availability of long term credit has always kept the French economy from developing its potential to the same degree that countries with basically British financial institutions have done.

The first American hyperinflation

A similar bubble popped at the same time in England, but by then Britain had become a stable constitutional monarchy that generally followed the sound principles of Dutch finance that William of Orange brought with him when he became King so that it avoided the chaotic financial conditions characteristic both of the earlier Stuart era and of contemporary France. The United States was probably saved from the worst effects of revolutionary finance by the fact that it was predominantly a nation of subsistence farmers so that the hyperinflation of the 1780's affected mainly a handful of merchants and bankers in the cities along the East Coast. Nevertheless, the experience left the American people with a respect for sound national finance that lasted for nearly a century and a half, and gave us the picturesque nickname shin-plaster for the currency issued by the revolutionary Continental Congress. In 1790 the Continental currency was redeemed by being exchanged for Government bonds at the rate of 100 Continental dollars for each 1 dollar principal amount of the new bonds.

Financial institutions and the credit system

I do not mean to imply that all financial disasters have been caused by irresponsible Government financial policy. Two of the great ones—the crash following the wild speculation in tulip bulbs in Holland during the 1630's and the South Seas bubble in Britain in 1720—both appear to have been primarily the results of rising private wealth and savings at a time when sound investment outlets were scarce and facilities for investigating proposed investments were virtually nonexistent. Indeed, throughout the eighteenth century as Britain grew steadily wealthier the country was almost constantly bedeviled by speculative promotions.

The answer to this problem emerged during the nineteenth century in the form of the enormous growth of financial institutions. The historical roots of modern financial institutions extend well back into the early years of the Renaissance, but until the end of the Napoleonic Wars in 1815 they were of interest primarily to the relatively few people who were involved with industry and commerce while the bulk of humanity was still engaged in subsistence farming. During the nineteenth century, however, the rapid growth of manufacturing industry and of commerce caused an enormous increase in human wealth, while the success of the European nations in acquiring colonies all over the world caused the great majority of the human race to be exposed to the latest political and financial practices to an unprecedented degree. Thus, in the years before World War I a worldwide financial system had evolved that was based upon the belief that money consisted essentially of coins or bullion that represented purchasing power because they were inherently valuable; but that had also developed a sophisticated and highly efficient method of investing in productive enterprises through the medium of financial promises to repay purchasing power in the future.

Before 1914 the monetary and the financial systems were compatible

Financial institutions were crucial to the working of this dual system in several respects. First, they accepted the individually small savings of people who were producing more than they were currently consuming and lumped them together into usefully large agglomerations of capital. Second, they retained staffs of professional investment experts whose function was to determine which of the various proposals for productive investments were in fact likely to increase human productivity by an amount sufficient to repay the savings invested in them along with a reasonable rent for their use. And, finally, they gave savers a reason to believe that the fruits of their own productive efforts that had been invested in productive enterprises through the medium of intangible promises to repay in the future still retained a real tangible value because the liabilities of financial institutions were generally payable either in the form of further financial promises or in the form of money with tangible value. In the normal course of events, and when confidence in the stability of the financial system was unshaken, creditors of financial institutions would usually draw checks upon their balance to pay their debts and to buy real goods and services; but if you ever got worried about the soundness of this complex system you could always go down to the bank and take out your balance in the form of precious metals.

If this arrangement had been deliberately and consciously devised it would have been hailed as a stroke of financial genius because it made inflation, in the modern sense of the word, mechanically infeasible. However, it simply evolved out of the efforts of practical men trying to find a better, easier and more profitable way of doing things. (In fact, most effective financial arrangements evolved in just that fashion.

Those that worked well were continued and those that didn't were abandoned.)

It worked spectacularly well; and indeed during the hundred years between the end of the Napoleonic Wars in 1815 and the outbreak of World War I in 1914 the general price level fell gently but persistently, leading in turn to a declining trend in interest rates that rewarded holders of long-term financial instruments with a large profit in nominal terms, and an even larger one in real terms.

Since then the inflationary overissue of financial claims has driven money with intrinsic value from the scene

If one takes August 1914 as marking the dividing line between them, the contrasts between the nineteenth and the twentieth centuries are striking. In many aspects of human affairs there has been a complete reversal of trend. For example, before 1914 colonization and the political and military leadership provided by Great Britain caused a progressive improvement in civil order and personal security throughout most of the world. After that year two world wars and the Cold War, which have left the world awash in arms, decolonization and the failure to maintain world leadership, first by Britain and then by the United States, have produced a disastrously declining trend in order and security that has already condemned millions of people to untimely and miserable deaths.

In the financial world, during the nineteenth century the existence of a monetary system based upon money that possessed intrinsic value alongside a financial system that mobilized the world's steadily growing savings and invested them in the construction of the productive facilities of industry and commerce stimulated a great increase in world prosperity, a declining general price level, and a considerable degree of long-run financial stability. (This longer term stability contrasted with occasional short-run financial crises or panics; their significance will be discussed later). In the twentieth century money with intrinsic value has disappeared completely. The financial system of intangible claims has continued to grow enormously, and has also continued to foster an increase of general prosperity in those parts of the world that are still sufficiently peaceful to make that possible; but it has also produced a wildly fluctuating and now sharply rising trend of prices, a wildly fluctuating and now sharply rising trend of interest rates, and rapidly increasing financial instability.

The disappearance of money with intrinsic value

There are many reasons for this fundamental change in the financial environment, several of which we will explore later; but clearly one major reason was the severance of the linkage between the financial system and money with intrinsic value that began in 1914. When the World War broke out many of the combatants suspended the convertibility of financial instruments into gold, and asked their citizens to surrender their precious metals in exchange for paper credit money, as measures of war finance. Once again, the consequences of financing war through irresponsible short-term borrowing, rather than through mobilizing the real savings of the people by selling them long-term bonds without permitting them to make offsetting increases in their short-term indebtedness, ranged from poor to cataclysmic. The countries that lost the war—Germany, Austria and Hungary—experienced ruinous hyperinflations during the next five years that destroyed the accumulated savings of the more stable elements of their societies, and that contributed greatly to the collapse of the democratic governments that were imposed upon them by the victorious Allied Powers. The ultimate consequences during the next quarter century included political and social chaos accompanied or followed by dictatorial governments, another world war, and another bout with hyperinflation during the 1940's.

In the United States the breaking of the linkage started

later and took longer than it did in Europe partly because the burden of World War I upon its financial system was not as great as it was in Europe, and partly because of the historical accident that it had a dual monetary system based both upon gold and upon silver. The United States went off gold internally in 1934 as part of a policy of deliberate "reflation," and it was forced off silver by a run on the Treasury's silver supplies that coincided with the onset of serious inflation in the mid-1960's. Externally the United States dollar remained formally convertible into gold until 1971, but after the mid-1960's only on the condition that nobody actually try to convert.

The breaking of the linkage was a momentous event. Before 1914 inflation was almost exclusively a war-related phenomenon.[2] Governments have almost never been willing to pay for wars entirely through open and above-board taxes and through mobilizing the real savings of their people by selling them long-term bonds without permitting them to borrow against the bonds. During the nineteenth century it was customary to "go off gold" at the outbreak of war, but to go back on it when peace and financial stability had been restored; and responsible governments tried to return to the gold value that their currency had had before the war started by offsetting the war's inflation with a peacetime deflation.

The case of the American Civil War is particularly instructive. After the country (the North, that is) went off gold and started printing paper money, inflation reduced its value to the point at which $2.33 in paper equaled $1.00 in gold in 1864. Nevertheless, the Federal Government was able to finance the war at an interest cost that ranged between 5 and 6 percent—very modest rates considering the inflation, the desperate nature of the war, and the initial uncertainty that the Union would win. Part of the reason was that Govern-

---

[2]Including revolution. The worst hyperinflations are usually associated with weak governments that either hang on by the skin of their teeth, as in the case of the German Government in 1923, or that fail to make it, as in the case of the Kuomintang Government of China in 1948.

ment bonds were valuable to banks as collateral backing up their own issues of bank notes.[3] More important was the fact that astute people expected that after the war gold convertibility would be restored at the prewar parity so that buying Government bonds with depreciated greenbacks would turn out to be very profitable in real terms; and by 1880 that is indeed the way it turned out. Can you imagine anyone, anywhere, today expecting any government to be that responsible?

"Money is by nature gold and silver."
—Karl Marx

By the mid-1960's the inflationary proliferation of credit instruments had, in accordance with Gresham's Law, driven money with intrinsic value off the financial scene by causing people to hoard coins and bullion, thereby making the convertibility of bank notes and other financial instruments impossible to maintain in the face of the growing demand for precious metals that could be trusted to at least maintain their real value. Virtually everything that we now use to settle transactions is an inconvertible financial instrument of one kind or another. The things that are called money today are simply the most liquid—that is, the most easily and conveniently spendable—of the financial instruments in the system. In the United States, for example, now that both the gold and the silver certificates are gone and gold and silver coins are carefully hoarded treasures, the dollars that remain are simply evidences of a non-interest-bearing debt of one or another of the regional Federal Reserve banks. Our present coins are simply tokens that look like the old silver coins, but that are usually worth much less as metal than their nominal

---

[3]You will better understand some of the points that are made later in this book if you are aware that issuing bank notes is profitable because they are in effect interest-free loans from the public to the bank, the proceeds of which are invested in Government bonds or other interest-bearing assets that act as collateral securing the loan. The price that the public pays for the high degree of liquidity that bank notes possess is the foregoing of income on its funds.

monetary value. (One exception is the copper penny, which occasionally causes a problem by becoming worth more as metal than as money.)

Money no longer exists

This fundamental change, without which the accelerating inflation and growing financial instability of the late 1960's and the 1970's would not have been possible, has received surprisingly little theoretical attention from respectable economists. (There are a number of people who consider the change to be of major importance, and who believe that financial stability cannot be restored until we "go back on gold," but most academic economists consider them to be rather disreputable characters. My own views on the vitally important question of how price and financial stability can be restored will be stated later, in Chapter 8.) One of the major theoretical consequences of the disappearance of money with intrinsic value is that the verbal distinction that we continue to make between money on the one hand and credit on the other no longer represents a real difference. I repeat that everything we use today to settle transactions is a credit instrument—an evidence of a debt. Therefore, I propose to banish the word "money" from our technical vocabulary. It stems from the Latin word moneta, which means coins[4]; and after more than two millennia of signifying intrinsic value it has connotations that are mischievous and misleading in a world from which real money has vanished altogether. A good substitute is the word "funds" which, at least in British usage, is associated with the concept of debt rather than that of money with intrinsic value. When we are talking less technically, as I will be doing in Chapter 7, the use of the word "money" is convenient, and does no harm

---

[4]A note for the etymologically inclined. Moneta in Latin originally meant an advisor, and it was a complimentary term applied to the goddess Juno, who was piously considered to be an advisor to the Roman state. It came to be associated with money because the Roman coins were minted in the temple of Juno the Advisor.

as long as we remember that its meaning has completely changed since 1914.

The German hyperinflation

One of the minor consequences of the failure to realize that once money with intrinsic value has gone the discrimination between money and credit becomes a distinction without a difference is that the catastrophic inflation that afflicted Germany between 1914 and 1923 is almost universally misinterpreted. It is generally considered to be a classic example of a printing press, paper money inflation. I maintain not only that the distinction between money and credit was obsolete in Germany after August 1914, but also that the enormous expansion of the nominal value of the bank notes outstanding was not a fundamental cause of the inflation. (It was, of course, a contributing factor that permitted the inflation to continue for longer than would otherwise have been possible.)

Before 1914 the German currency consisted both of gold coins and of Reichsbank notes that, like all self-respecting nineteenth century paper currencies, were freely exchangeable for gold. Under the terms of the Bank Law of 1875, which was still in force in 1914, the Reichsbank had to maintain a gold reserve equal to at least one-third of its notes outstanding. The rest of the backing for the currency could consist of three months commercial bills that were supposed to finance physical inventories of real goods that were moving through the distribution system toward the ultimate buyers, and those bills had to be guaranteed by reputable businessmen in order to be eligible as collateral securing the Reichsbank's note issue. It was expected that the Reichsbank's holdings of these bills would fluctuate seasonally and cyclically as the Reichsbank discharged its responsibility for financing the short-term requirements of the business community. These provisions are typical of both the theory and the practice of the nineteenth-century financial system that was based both upon money with intrinsic value and upon credit that was intended to finance real productive activity; the financial stability of the system being assured by the convertibility of financial assets into money with intrinsic value.

1914 marked a radical, and in the end catastrophic, transformation of that system. At the beginning of the war the Germans expected it to last for six weeks, after which they would make the French pay for it in the form of reparations in gold, and perhaps physical goods, as they had done after the Franco-Prussian war. Therefore, they viewed the question of war finance as a matter of dealing with a short-run emergency that would not require a major mobilization of the real savings of the German people. So the first steps that were taken in August were essentially temporary expedients. The convertibility of Reichsbank notes into gold was suspended, and people were exhorted to turn in their gold marks for paper ones as a patriotic duty. The Reichsbank was authorized to issue bank notes secured by Treasury bills as collateral (that is, to make unlimited short-term loans to the Government)—something that had not been permitted previously—and new loan banks were established to make loans to governmental bodies, to war contractors and for the purchase of war bonds. The notes of these new banks were to circulate as legal tender. Thus the war was financed not primarily by taxes and the investment of real savings in long-term bonds, but by short-term borrowings. After 1916 taxes were raised, but the revenue they produced was very small. More than 60 percent of total German Government expenditures during the war years were financed by borrowings. The consequence was that both the internal and the external value of the mark fell by about one-half between the beginning of 1914 and the beginning of 1919. The German standard of living also declined by about the same amount. Undoubtedly one of the reasons why Germany lost the war was that the servicemen, who were on fixed pay, knew that they would come out of it poor men.

The Armistice, and the subsequent Treaty of Versailles, required Germany to surrender a vast amount of war materiel, including a great deal of badly needed transportation equipment, stripped the country not only of its colonies but also of about one-seventh of its domestic territory including some of its most productive industrial and agricultural regions, and also required that the German army be rapidly shrunk by 75 percent. These provisions would have caused a further fall in the German standard of living and created a massive unemployment problem, in a country whose social fabric had already been severely strained, even without the added burden of reparations. On top of all that the Treaty of Versailles required that the German Federal Government be democratic, and that it guarantee democratic government to each of the constituent states. (I am using the word "states" in its American signification. The equivalent German word is länder.)

Now, the question of political democracy had been settled in the negative in Germany by the failure of the 1848 revolution after which German political democrats emigrated to the United States where they did many useful things, including the founding of the Guardian Life Insurance Company of America in 1860.[5]

The net result was that a weak and unpopular government had to attempt to deal with the problems of an impoverished and disorganized country that was already suffering a serious inflation that had been caused by irresponsible war finance, and that had also had an enormous external debt imposed upon it. The situation was further complicated by the fact that Germany had had no significant experience of inflation before 1914, and so most people completely failed to understand what was happening. They thought that the prices of goods were going up because of the Allied blockade during the war and the postwar anti-German machinations of the Allies, not that the value of the mark was going down.

Weak governments faced with intractable problems generally believe that they must create all the purchasing power that the market demands. Since it is much easier to create purchasing power than it is to create real goods and services

---

[5]Until 1917 the Company was called the Germania Life Insurance Company of America. The present name results from the fact that its home office, which was completed in 1911, is full of expensive marble that is deeply carved with the initials G.L.I. Co.

available to be purchased the inevitable result is inflation, which politicians blame on anything and everything but their own financial policies. The Weimar Government was no exception. There were the Allies to blame, and the external depreciation of the mark that resulted from the fact that Germany was running a balance of payments deficit and making large payments abroad at a time when astute international traders and foreign exchange dealers realized that the viability of postwar Germany was doubtful in the extreme. As a matter of fact, between the end of the war and the final collapse late in 1923 the external value of the mark fell faster than its internal value so that Germany was a bargain hunter's paradise for anyone with access to foreign funds.

Certainly the President of the Reichsbank, Dr. Rudolf Havenstein, believed that the constant rise of both domestic and import prices made it imperative to maintain German purchasing power by increasing the supply of money and credit correspondingly, and he boasted of the efficiency of his presses in cranking out bank notes. This attempt to maintain some reasonable part of the nation's real purchasing power by continuously accelerating the creation of nominal purchasing power failed dismally. By the time that total disaster impended, during the dark days of the Ruhrkampf,[6] the

[6]At the beginning of 1923 the French occupied the Ruhr in order to collect the reparations that the Germans had not paid out of the production of that coal mining and industrial region. The Germans were in no position to resist the occupation by military measures, so they decided to frustrate the French by means of a general strike supported by transfer payments from the rest of the country. It was this attempt, on the part of a nation already impoverished by a decade of war and postwar disorganization, to support 6 million people in unproductive idleness, that pushed Germany over the brink into hyperinflation. It is worth mentioning that unproductivity is not always this obvious. In post–World War I Austria, where financial catastrophe developed even more rapidly than it did in Germany, all of the Government employees were kept on the payroll even though it was now the Government of a Republic of 6½ million people instead of the prewar Empire of 50 million. I will note later that much of the efforts of the current United States Government employees are downright counterproductive. For an informative account of the hyperinflation in Central Europe, see Adam Fergusson, *When Money Dies*, William Kimber and Company, Ltd., London, 1975.

real value of the average wage had fallen to perhaps 20 percent of the 1913 level, and clearly to below the subsistence level. However, the real value of the currency in circulation had fallen to about 3 percent of the 1913 level.[7] The increase in the nominal value of the currency in circulation was fantastic, but the inflation proceeded even faster. The velocity of circulation approached its physically possible limit as workers were paid daily, and given the next half hour off to spend the money; but in fact during the last few years of the inflation there was a chronic shortage of money because it could not be printed fast enough. Municipal governments were authorized to print their own emergency money; and toward the end many businesses that enjoyed a good local credit standing printed their own money illegally because they had to pay their workers with something. Moreover, when stabilization came the printing of money did *not* stop—during the following months the supply of legally authorized money multiplied several times again, but prices stabilized and then fell sharply.

It seems quite clear that the chief cause of the German hyperinflation was not the increase in the money supply, fantastic though that was, but the ready availability of credit first to finance the war and then to finance the inflation hedging that developed on an enormous scale once astute people began to realize what was going on. In 1922 and 1923 the Reichsbank rediscounted everybody's notes freely, and at an interest rate of 5 percent per annum until July 1922. After that it raised the rediscount rate by steps up to 90 percent per annum in September 1923—when the inflation rate was on the order of 25 percent *per day*. I have found the clearest account of the dynamics of the situation not in any Economics textbook, but in the novel *The Black Obelisk*, by the German author Erich Maria Remarque[8]:

---

[7]By 1923 the currency in circulation corresponded to the m_1 definition of the money supply. Checks were no longer accepted because the real value of the sum involved would fall disastrously during the few days it took for the check to clear.

[8]From pages 54 and 55 of THE BLACK OBELISK, © 1957, by Erich Maria Remarque. Reprinted by permission of Harcourt Brace Jovanovich, Inc.

On the day he receives the note from us he must take it to his bank or ours and have it discounted. The bank ascertains that both Riesenfeld and we are good for its face value, deducts a few percent for discounting the note, and pays out the money. We pay back Riesenfeld the amount of the bank's commission. Thus, he receives full payment for the shipment just as though we had paid in advance. Nor does the bank lose. It immediately sends the note to the Reichsbank, which in turn pays just as the bank paid Riesenfeld. And there in the Reichsbank it remains until, on the expiration date, it is presented for payment. What it will be worth then is easy to imagine. We have only known about all this since 1922. Before then. . . . we had sold out almost our entire inventory and, to our amazement had nothing to show for it except a worthless bank account and a few suitcases full of currency not even good enough to paper our walls with. We tried at first to sell and then buy again as quickly as possible—but the inflation easily overtook us. The lag before we got paid was too long; while we waited, the value of money fell so fast that even our most profitable sale turned into a loss. Only after we began to pay with promissory notes could we maintain our position. Even so, we are making no real profit now, but at least we can live. Since every enterprise in Germany is financed in this fashion, the Reichsbank naturally has to keep on printing unsecured currency and so the mark falls faster and faster. The government apparently doesn't care; all it loses in this way is the national debt. Those who are ruined are the people who cannot pay with notes, the people who have property they are forced to sell, small shopkeepers, day laborers, people with small incomes who see their private savings and their bank accounts melting away, and government officials and employees who have to survive on salaries that no longer allow them to buy so much as a new pair of shoes. The ones who profit are the exchange kings, the profiteers, the foreigners who buy what they like with a few dollars, kronen, or zlotys, and the big entrepreneurs, the manufacturers, and the speculators on the exchange whose property and stocks increase without limit. For them practically everything is free. It is the great sellout of thrift, honest effort, and respectability. The vultures flock from all sides, and the only ones who come out on top are those who accumulate debts. The debts disappear of themselves.

This passage reflects the situation in April 1923, before the

Ruhrkampf really began to bite. It was this extra burden that turned what had long been a desperate situation into a disaster. By late 1923 urban Germany was beginning to starve because its wage earners were being paid in a rapidly depreciating credit money that the farmers would no longer accept in exchange for food. The signs of imminent collapse were everywhere. Government revenue now covered 3 percent or less of expenditure. The Ruhr was full of mobs of desperate looters, and violent crime was rising throughout the country.

At the end of September the Government recognized that it would have to abandon the Ruhrkampf; and the realization that the struggle and sacrifice had been in vain touched off a political crisis that threatened to tear Germany apart. Separatist movements broke out in several parts of the country, and those in Saxony and Thuringia had to be put down by military force. Hitler sensed that the bottom had been reached, and staged his unsuccessful putsch in Munich on November 8.

The stabilization

It was in this disastrous situation that Dr. Hjalmar Schacht became Commissioner for the National Currency on November 13, and he had no attempt at a "soft landing" out of inflation. A new bank had been established to issue a currency called the rentenmark that was secured by corporate bonds and real estate mortgages. One rentenmark was declared to be equal in value to one prewar gold mark, and the farmers believed it even though it was actually just another inconvertible bank note. The threat of starvation receded as farmers began to ship food to the cities again. Schacht also insisted that the discounting of Treasury bills be stopped forthwith, and two days later it was stopped.

On November 20 (by a curious coincidence, the day on which Dr. Havenstein died) the mark declined to one-billionth of its prewar value against the dollar (that is in the European system of counting—one-million-millionth). That made the arithmetic simple, and so the mark was stabilized by striking off twelve zeroes. 1,000,000,000,000 paper marks were declared to be equal in value to 1 new rentenmark, and therefore notionally to one of the gold marks with which ten years earlier they had been interchangeable.

The stabilization of the external value of the mark was easily accomplished by the simple but drastic step of making credit unavailable to finance foreign exchange speculation. At that time financial transactions in Germany were settled at the end of the month. Toward the end of November the exchange rate on the free market was 12 billion marks[9] to the dollar, but the official rate was 4⅕ billion marks to the dollar. At the end of the month, when speculators came to the Reichsbank to borrow the marks that they had sold short at twelve billion to the dollar Dr. Schacht refused to make them available; and so they had to cover, either by using their dollar balances to buy marks from the Reichsbank at 4⅕ billion to the dollar, or by making the best deal they could on the free market. This sudden and unexpected demand to buy marks with foreign currencies sent their external value soaring. The steady flow of new credit that was required to support the over-leveraged corporate conglomerations that had been acquired by inflation-hedgers like Hugo Stinnes was also cut off, and they promptly collapsed.

Thus the inflation was halted *not* by stopping the presses that were printing bank notes, but by a cold turkey policy of abruptly cutting off the flow of new credit to the Government and the market. Once the stabilization took hold deflation was inevitable because the people and businesses that had survived that long had done so by borrowing to the hilt in the expectation that inflation would wipe out the real burden of their debts. In terms of stable prices the economy was fantastically over-indebted, and very few of the successful inflation hedges survived the succeeding deflation. Their collapse caused severe unemployment, but at least the total disaster toward which Germany was headed in 1923 was averted.

[9]That is in the American system of counting, according to which a billion is a thousand million. In Europe a thousand million is called a milliard.

During the next few years various attempts were made to tax away a bit of the profits that debtors had realized from the destruction of the German financial system and to restore to creditors a trifle of the purchasing power that they had lost. Nevertheless, for all practical purposes the savings that had been held in the form of intangible financial claims were wiped out. The next quarter century in Germany was catastrophic, but it is not possible to sort out the contribution of the collapse of the financial system from those of all the other disasters that Germany had experienced during the preceding decade. In Chapter 5 we will take a look at the contributions that the financial system makes to human welfare when it is functioning properly.

What it is that gets borrowed and lent

The point of this review of nineteenth and early twentieth century financial history is that our present financial system only makes sense in terms of reasonably stable prices, but its great efficiency makes it very easy to produce a destabilizing and inflationary overexpansion of credit. During the nineteenth century there existed two conditions that tended to prevent such an inflationary overexpansion of credit. One of them we have already discussed. It was the convertibility of financial instruments into money with intrinsic value. The last remaining vestiges of that were driven from the financial scene by the inflationary proliferation of credit instruments in the mid-1960's; and it is unlikely to return unless a wholesale financial smash forces us to start over from the beginning, as the Germans did at the end of 1923, and again in 1948. The other condition, which will be discussed later, could be restored much more easily by simply reversing some of the twentieth century trends that have overwhelmed it.

Meanwhile, what is it that gets borrowed and lent, if it is not money? The answer that it is credit instruments is correct, but not very enlightening. At bottom, what the creditor lends—and hopes to get back—is the real purchasing power that he has earned by his productive efforts; but the best that the twentieth-century financial system can guarantee him is nominal purchasing power. The gap between the two can, if it widens much further, destroy both the financial system and the wealth of its creditors.

Some of the theoretical consequences of recognizing that money no longer exists

One consequence of recognizing that nothing that is properly called money exists any longer is that we can get rid of the proliferation of m's (m_1, m_{1+}, m_2 . . .), which is getting out of hand, and start making some more useful distinctions between the various kinds of credit instruments. The meaningful problem that all the m's are clumsy attempts to solve is that of defining different degrees of liquidity, but attempting to solve it in terms of an obsolete distinction between money on the one hand and credit on the other is not very helpful. When you try to draw a sharp qualitative line across what is in fact a continuous spectrum that is best approached in quantitative terms, you naturally run into a problem about just where to put the line; and it is that artificial problem that has produced the plethora of m's.[10]

Liquidity is the crucial factor, not the money supply

The degree of liquidity that financial instruments possess is vitally important both to the holders of those instruments and to the financial and political Authorities. Liquidity is

---

[10]In order to be fair, I must note that some advanced monetarists are stumbling toward enlightenment on this point because they are beginning to realize that m_7—all liquid financial instruments—is the monetary aggregate that works the best. At that point our views converge for practical purposes, but I still think that it is more accurate to say that everything we now use as money is a credit instrument than it is to call all credit instruments money.

important to the holders of financial instruments because it measures the degree of ease and convenience with which they can be turned back into ready purchasing power, and the degree of certainty that their holders are justified in feeling about just how much real purchasing power they represent. Thus, the more liquid a financial instrument is the more likely it is to be spent. Liquidity is also important to the Authorities because prices will remain stable only if the society as a whole spends just about as much as it produces. If its spending rises more rapidly than the output of real goods and services expands, the general price level will rise; and if its spending rises less rapidly, either real output or the general price level or both will have to drop. The likelihood that people will spend the savings that they hold in the form of financial instruments is greatly influenced by the liquidity of those instruments, and thus it is vitally important that the overall liquidity of the financial system be appropriate. If the system is too liquid people will tend to spend excessively and inflation will be a problem; but if it is insufficiently liquid the need of some people to spend the savings that they hold in the form of relatively illiquid financial instruments, and of other people to liquidate investments in order to get the wherewithal to repay maturing debts, will cause the market prices of the less liquid instruments to decline. If this process goes far enough it may cause a liquidity crisis, which is also called a financial panic.

The assets of financial institutions are less liquid, but produce a larger income, than their liabilities

Since savers usually want to be able to recapture their purchasing power easily and are willing to forgo some income to maintain liquidity while people and businesses who borrow and invest in productive assets want to be sure of having the purchasing power as long as they need it and are willing to pay some additional interest to get it, one of the functions of financial institutions is to accommodate both of them by accepting relatively liquid but also relatively low cost deposits as their liabilities, and investing them in less liquid but higher yielding financial assets. As a broad generalization, liquidity and income vary inversely with each other. The earnings of financial institutions arise primarily from the spread between the interest rates that they earn and those that they pay. Those earnings represent the value of the service that they render to savers and to borrowers by assuming the risks involved in holding assets that are less liquid than their liabilities.

The obsolete distinction between money and credit should be replaced by an accurate measure of degrees of liquidity

As the financial system evolved, it developed a wide variety of financial instruments that by now constitute a broad and continuous spectrum with respect to liquidity and yield. One end of the spectrum is represented by bank notes (in the United States, Federal Reserve notes that are called dollar bills) that are almost completely liquid but that yield no income at all. The other end of the spectrum is represented by the bonds and notes of small businesses that have only a local reputation, or the bonds of obscure municipalities that are traded only by the local bank but that provide a good income that is not taxed by the Federal, State, or local Government.

The degree of liquidity a financial instrument possesses is not always accurately determinable until you actually try to spend it because it depends to some extent on the surrounding circumstances. For example, a million dollar Treasury bill is easily spendable in any financial center during business hours, but if you want to buy gasoline at two o'clock in the morning Federal Reserve notes in small denominations will work better. Nevertheless, the liquidity of the various kinds of financial instruments issued by recognized borrowers lends itself reasonably well to quantitative treatment. I propose that we replace the cumbersome array of m's with the tidier system of a schedule of liquidity values.

The velocity of the circulation of bank notes is not particularly important

Another cumbersome theoretical concept that we can also dispose of is the notion of the velocity of the circulation of money, for the good and simple reason that there is nothing left to apply it to. The conventional theory is that the general price level is determined by the formula $MV = PT$, in which M is the quantity of money in circulation, V is the velocity with which it passes from hand to hand, T is the number of transactions occurring in the period of time under review, and P is the resulting price level. The formula may be useful in extreme cases like the German hyperinflation, when we have some independent information about the rate of circulation of bank notes; but in general it is an obsolete way of looking at things that lost its usefulness when there ceased to be a meaningful difference between money and credit. Today it is more important to recognize that the general price level will remain stable when credit is created no more rapidly than the real economy will respond with an equivalent increase in the output of real goods and services, and when credit is used primarily to finance real productive investments that will increase the productivity of human efforts by a sufficient amount to justify forgoing current consumption in order to make them.

There is no such thing as a stable rate of inflation

Once we recognize clearly that all the things that get lent and spent in modern economies are financial instruments, which are promises to repay in the future that were issued at some time in the past in exchange for then-current purchasing power, and that there no longer exists any limit to the ability of the financial system to create financial claims corresponding to the limit that was imposed upon the financial systems of the nineteenth century by the creditors' ability to exchange financial instruments for money that possessed intrinsic value, it is easy to see why inflation has become such an intractable problem. First, most of us are more fond of the purchasing power than we are of the work that is involved in earning it by producing real goods and services. Second, in political democracies the way to get elected to political office is to promise the people more of the unearned purchasing power that can be created by the apparently magical and effortless process of debt formation than your opponent does. Third, social democracy asserts that incomes are deserved as a matter of right whether or not we produce real goods and services; and the only way that incomes can be produced out of thin air, without the effort and bother of producing real goods and services, is through debt formation—at the cost of inflation. Finally, once practical people grasp the implications of all this and decide that inflation is here to stay, they rush to borrow as heavily as they can in order to buy real things whose prices they hope will at least keep up with the inflation. Thus a self-sustaining spiral is generated that has the capacity to continue and to accelerate indefinitely as long as credit remains generally available. Once inflation has become endemic the *only* sure way to stop it is to limit the creation of new credit to the amount that is likely to be used for real productive investment. The question of just how that can be accomplished, in the absence of money with intrinsic value, will be taken up in Chapter 8.

The last point mentioned, borrowing to buy inflation hedges, is not clearly recognized in current financial theory even though it is by now the biggest financial game in town. That process and its implications will be examined in the next chapter.

FOUR

Why Inflation Produces Financial Disasters

A new motive for economic behavior

The expectation of rising prices that results from the experience of endemic inflation creates a new motive for economic behavior. Once inflation has set in and is expected to continue, people borrow in order to buy things whose prices they expect to at least keep up with the inflation; and those things are typically either equities in existing businesses or tangible objects, the prices of which are expected to rise because they are *unique* and *irreplaceable*, and therefore by definition not available out of current production. American industry can turn out power tools by the millions; therefore their prices have not gone up much in recent years, and they appear to be relative bargains. But nobody will ever paint another Rembrandt. Waterfront property and real estate in general, art objects, antiques of all kinds—these are the typical inflation hedges. Debt that is created to buy existing inflation hedges has no immediate impact upon real output, only upon prices. However, in recent years Americans have also borrowed heavily against the equity in their houses in order to finance purchases of durable consumer goods; and this has had a substantial and largely unpredicted impact upon real output. Failure to foresee this phenomenon, or to grasp its significance when it began to happen, is one of the reasons why many economists consistently underestimated the strength and durability of the economic expansion of 1975–1979.

Unfortunately, fads in inflation hedges develop and cause too much debt to be incurred in the process of pushing the prices of the currently popular inflation hedges up to an unsustainable level. Then the next period of credit stringency causes a crash that damages or destroys their plausibility as inflation hedges, and the fad moves on to something else. We have had several examples of such localized financial disasters since inflation became endemic in the United States during the mid-1960's.

Localized financial disasters

I was personally involved in the first example, which is an arithmetically clear one although it will seem a little obscure to readers who are not intimately familiar with the financial markets. In the summer of 1965 I joined the outstanding bond firm Salomon Brothers (& Hutzler, as it was then) as a convertible bond analyst. One of the first talks I gave to institutional customers was at Thanksgiving that year when Harry Brown, the partner in charge of the firm's Chicago office, asked me to address a luncheon for their customers in Minneapolis. Misunderstanding the nature of the occasion, I prepared an elaborate arithmetical analysis of the price of the typical convertible debenture that demonstrated that converts were completely unattractive for a buyer who was prepared to pay cash. Convertible bonds are supposed to (and at reasonable prices they do) combine much of the appreciation potential of the common stock into which they are convertible with a "floor" provided by their value as a claim to a stream of interest payments, with the repayment of the principal at the end. They normally sell at some premium both over their value as a call on the stock and over their value as a fixed-income security; but I argued that by late 1965 both of those premiums had grown so large that in the next bear market converts could easily fall *more* than their related common stocks—particularly if that bear market was caused by what we would now call a "credit crunch" (the term hadn't been invented in 1965), as I rather expected.

Convertible bonds were designed to be less vulnerable than their related commons, but their prices had advanced so much more than those of the stocks had since the bonds were issued that the premiums had become excessive for the cash buyer. I attributed the excess to the fact that margin speculators who were on good terms with their bankers could borrow up to 90 percent or so of their market value, at a time when the maximum that it was legal to borrow to buy stocks was 30 percent of the market value; and the greater leverage available on converts meant that a good upward move in the stock would produce a much larger profit on the bond than was legally possible if you held the stock on margin. I called this excess premium over what it would be reasonable for the cash buyer to pay the collateral-value premium, and I suggested that institutional investors stay away from convertible bonds until it subsided because it made them vulnerable not only to a bear market in stocks, or to an increase in interest rates that would reduce the market value of bonds, but also to the possibility that the Fed might put minimum margin requirements on them also, which would shrink or destroy the collateral-value premium.

Harry Brown was heard to mutter into his drink that this was the strangest approach to selling bonds that he had ever run into, but the firm printed the talk and sent it to all its institutional customers; and a year later when all of those things had happened and I said that convertible bonds now appeared to be very cheap and attractive, I had considerable credibility. However, after they crashed in 1966 convertible bonds in general never recovered to the high prices at which they had sold in 1965.

During the later 1960's, after the Fed had spoiled the leverage game in convertible bonds, the thing to do to stay ahead of inflation was to buy common stocks. The leverage that is a requisite quality of an inflation hedge was added partly by margin buyers, but much more importantly by the corporate acquirers and conglomerators who were borrowing heavily in order to buy up the equity in other companies without issuing more of their own stock so that their earnings per share would be increased by the transaction. In 1967 and 1968 no one wanted to think about the overall implications of the acquisition boom, or to recognize the fact that this wholesale retirement of equities in exchange for debt was seriously undermining the financial condition of the business community as a whole. At the time I was managing pension funds for a large industrial corporation that was heavily involved in the acquisitions game, and the forecast for 1969 that is reprinted in the appendix to this book was an attempt to scare the top management into a more cautious strategy. During the next year and a half the impact of a stringent monetary policy upon the seriously overborrowed corporate sector produced another localized financial crisis, and a crash in stock prices from which they also have not yet entirely recovered.

The next plausible inflation hedge was commercial real estate; and in a remarkably short period of time a brand new financial industry—the real estate investment trusts, many of which specialized in buying real estate on as thin a margin as possible—grew to enormous size before the credit crunch of 1974–1975 brought it crashing down.

These localized financial disasters affected primarily businessmen and investors, and left the ordinary American relatively unscathed. The latest inflation-hedging fad looks much more ominous to me. Before 1976 the ordinary American apparently believed that accelerating inflation simply made the future outlook more dangerous and uncertain, so that as the inflation rate rose he tended to increase his savings as a percentage of his income. However, since then he also has begun to bet on inflation. The increase in mortgage debt on homes in 1974 was $35 billion, and in 1975 it was $40 billion. In 1976 it was $64 billion, in 1977 $96 billion, and in

1978 it was probably around $100 billion. The increase in home mortgage debt plus consumer debt in 1974 was $45 billion, and in 1975 it was $50 billion. By 1977 it had jumped to $130 billion, and in 1978 to about $150 billion. The current fad in inflation hedges is now houses; and I see no reason why the next credit squeeze should not produce the same results for house prices that each of the other credit crunches since 1966 has produced for the then-current inflation-hedging fad. In my judgment, the personal sector of the American economy is now clearly overindebted, and that fact bodes ill for the next economic downturn.

FIVE

The Social Value of the Financial System

The nature of the private financial system

Our present financial system facilitates two enormously valuable kinds of transfers of purchasing power. First, it enables people who are currently producing more purchasing power than they need or desire to consume at the moment to transfer the surplus to other people, businesses or governments who have an opportunity to invest it profitably in the machines, tools, roads, bridges and other facilities that make human efforts more efficient and productive. The resulting increase in human productivity allows the borrowers to pay a rent to the lenders for the use of their purchasing power. Thus the financial system improves human efficiency by transferring resources from savers to investors who use them to buy productive real assets.

The financial system also makes it possible to transfer purchasing power through time, and thereby enables people to make provision for their own future needs and responsibilities by allowing savers to use their current excess of purchasing power to buy financial claims that can later be reexchanged for goods and services that will be produced at some future time. Thus the financial system, as it exists today, not only provides claims against future production but also finances the investment in real productive resources that will be required to fulfill those claims in real terms when they are presented for payment. Whether it will continue to do so tomorrow is becoming increasingly doubtful.

The financial system provides two incidental benefits that are of considerable importance in themselves. First, it supplies financial instruments that function as media of exchange and that permit each of us to concentrate our efforts upon whatever it is that we do best and to exchange the fruits of our labors for financial claims that we can then use to buy all the wide variety of goods and services that we need and desire. Second, the rent that borrowers are willing to pay to obtain additional purchasing power, beyond that which they are creating by their own productive efforts, from savers who are not presently consuming as much as they are producing, sets a market value upon the deferral of consumption that provides a rational basis for deciding which investments are worth deferring consumption to make and which are not. An investment that does not appear to be likely to increase the productivity of human efforts by an amount sufficient to repay its cost, along with the going rate of interest until the cost is repaid, is not worth making; and the private financial markets, if they are left to their own devices, will not permit it to be made.

On the other hand, a point that is frequently overlooked these days is that financial institutions exist for the purpose of mobilizing savings and putting them to productive use. If an investment does appear to be sound, and likely to return at least the going rate of interest, it almost always can and will be financed. If mortgage lenders do in fact "redline," an assertion with respect to which empirical investigators can find very little hard evidence, it is not because they are evil or prejudiced but because they believe that the prospects for certain neighborhoods are too doubtful to justify the investment of their depositors' or policyholders' savings.

The simple fact, which everybody knows but nobody

wants to talk about, is that large residential areas in and near many of our cities are rapidly being destroyed. This is a consequence of one or both of two politically popular, but practically disastrous, policies. The first is rent control, an insanity that has already caused large parts of New York City to resemble nothing so much as Berlin in 1946, but that nonetheless is growing in political appeal west of the Hudson River as the inflation eats into the real standard of living of people with modest or relatively fixed incomes. The other is the combination of transfer payments and a legally mandated minimum wage that is well above the market value of the productive efforts that a large number of Americans, particularly those who were educated in the public schools of some of our large cities, are now capable of. The pretense that the minimum wage is a social good is an even more cruel hoax than the pretense that rent control is a benefit to the people who must live in the neighborhoods that it is destroying. The minimum wage does not raise the living standard of the marginally productive, it makes them unemployable; and while social democrats doubtless find the old adage that the devil finds work for idle hands ideologically distasteful, its truth is also beyond doubt. The concentration of idle people, who have no connection with the productive economy except transfer payments, in neighborhoods that the combination of rent control and inflation is destroying, makes those areas both depressing and dangerous to live in. This trend has implications for your own future that we will explore in the last chapter.

A further point with respect to housing that we will return to later is that it is not an investment in productive facilities, but is one of the cases in which borrowing to increase personal comfort and satisfaction is justified because otherwise very few of us could afford a place to live. However, speaking as a financial analyst, it is my view that the investment made in housing in the United States during the 1970's was clearly excessive. It has already caused a series of localized crises in state and municipal government finance, and it appears to be about to produce a national disaster. In my judgment, mortgage lending has become an extremely risky business in many areas; and in this connection I wish that politicians would remember that the funds that investment managers lend are not our own, nor do they really belong to the institutions that employ us. They are the savings of productive, self-reliant people who are attempting to provide for their own future needs and responsibilities. We are responsible to them for the prudent and profitable investment of their funds; and it is because I interpret my responsibilities broadly that I am writing this book to demonstrate that the attempt to provide for personal responsibilities is in rapidly increasing danger of being rendered fruitless by the consequences of political finance.

Political finance

Today it is increasingly common for politicians to cause things to be done, either through subsidies or mandates, that the private markets, left to themselves, would not do. It is true that there are some things, like providing police, military and fire protection, that are desirable for society as a whole to do but that would not be economic for any one person, business or institution to attempt on its own; and these are the proper functions of government. However, when politicians substitute their judgment for that of the financial market, and lend the credit of the State to projects that would not be financeable on their own merits, the record does not suggest that they are very likely to be right.

Unwise government investments always depress the real standard of living, below what it would have been if the investment had been made in something more useful, by wasting or misallocating resources and human efforts; and if they also cause the total volume of credit formation to be excessive they will produce inflation. In the case of nonsovereign governments that cannot declare their notes to be legal tender, they can also cause a local financial crisis. In 1975 and 1976 the State and City of New York and the Commonwealth of Massachusetts underwent such crises, largely because they provided excessive financing for subsidized housing.

The New York City situation illustrates the compounding effects of a variety of politically expedient but practically disastrous policies. After the crisis developed the City attempted to raise funds on the security of its mortgages on Mitchell-Lama subsidized housing projects, and one of our mortgage officers and I went to inspect some of them. A quick look around the neighborhoods made the fundamental process abundantly clear. First, many years of rent control had reduced the revenues from privately owned apartment houses to below their operating costs so that the owners abandoned them rather than suffer an out of pocket loss. Then people with nothing better to do moved in and wrecked them so that they became uninhabitable. Then, as long as its credit lasted, the City bulldozed them and replaced them with new apartments whose rents are subsidized out of tax revenues. Whether the new apartments are more desirable than the old ones is perhaps a question of aesthetics—most of the ones that we saw waiting to be demolished were substantial and spacious old brownstones that I would have preferred to the new ones—but the waste of resources, in a city that has little to spare, is appalling. By now the credit of New York City has been completely destroyed, and during the foreseeable future it will be able to finance only on the strength of a pledge of specific revenues (virtually all of which have already been hocked) or by the loan of the credit of the United States (or possibly that of New York State, but its creditworthiness at the moment is also rather shaky). New York City, like Great Britain, provides a preview, which it would be wise to heed, of what will happen to the entire country if the basic trend of national policy is not reversed.

The financial system is based upon the concept of personal responsibility

A major and recurring theme of this book is that there is a fundamental incompatibility between the financial system, as it presently exists, and the political finance that almost inevitably accompanies the attempt to socialize the function of providing for future needs and responsibilities. Savers are people who are attempting to provide for their own future needs, and for their family responsibilities, out of the fruits of their own labors. That is something that was not easily possible for most people to accomplish until large and sound financial institutions became available to them during the nineteenth century; and it is something that may cease to be possible during our lifetime. Throughout most of humanity's hunting and agrarian history the only effective form of old-age security that was available to most people was to have children who would support them in their later years; and the only forms of accumulated wealth that could be passed along from one generation to the next were tools, livestock and the family farm. The current system of holding wealth in the form of intangible financial claims—stocks, bonds, mortgages, bankbooks, life insurance policies and the like—is a comparative novelty for most of humanity, and if we continue to abuse it as badly as we have been doing during most of the last two decades it is entirely possible that it will collapse and disappear from the human scene.

That would be a tragedy, for the development of the present financial system was, in practical terms, one of the greatest advances in human freedom that has ever been made. It broke the bonds of dependency between the generations. Today people who have become unproductive because of age, but who have worked responsibly and conducted their affairs prudently, usually have accumulated sufficient financial claims to support themselves without being a burden upon their children. Similarly, young people are now usually free to pursue their own interests and prospects without the handicap of having to support their parents or grandparents. That handicap may not have been substantial for farmers who owned their own land, but in our contemporary mobile and urban society it could be crippling. However, today that ancient dependence of the aged upon the productive young is beginning to reemerge, in a slightly modified form, as a consequence of the inadequate financing of social insurance schemes; and the political attempt to push the consequences of that reemergence as far off into the future as possible is likely to intensify the inflationary pressures that have already resulted from more general causes.

Responsible finance versus political finance

The basic financial problem facing us today is that during the last half century or so the financial system, which originally developed out of the efforts of individuals to provide effectively for their own needs and responsibilities, has been increasingly bent and reshaped by political forces to serve further social goals with which it is not entirely compatible; and in the process the sense of financial responsibility that is required to keep it functioning satisfactorily is progressively breaking down. Consider the difference between the ways in which responsible financial institutions like the Guardian Life Insurance Company on the one hand, and the Federal Old Age and Survivors and Disability Insurance System on the other, prepare to meet a responsibility. Whenever we promise to make a payment to someone in the future we set up a fund, called a reserve, that, compounding at a very modest rate of interest, will be sufficient to fulfill that promise when it becomes payable; and we invest that fund in a project that we believe will increase the productivity of human efforts by an amount sufficient to repay the principal and at least the assumed rate of interest on the reserves, with an additional margin of profit for the borrower if all goes well and a margin of safety for the lender if it does not. This kind of promise does not have an inflationary impact upon the general price level because it is initially funded out of real savings, by which I mean income that could have been but was not spent upon consumption, and it is invested in facilities that increase human productivity. Politicians, on the other hand, regularly make large promises of future benefits without setting any significant amount aside to fund them because they intend to pay the benefits when they come due out of taxes upon future productive efforts.

Even though no significant amount of financial or real assets have been accumulated to make good on those promises, nevertheless it is reasonable for each individual person who is covered by Social Security to count on the future income that he has been promised (as long as he does not believe that the United States Government is likely to renege on its promises—we will return to this point later) and to reduce proportionately the savings that he is accumulating out of his own earned income to provide for his future needs and responsibilities. Dr. Martin Feldstein, a Professor of Economics at Harvard University, has estimated that the existence of the pay-as-you-go Social Security system has reduced our national savings rate by about 50 percent, and is thus largely responsible for the low rate of real investment in this country that has caused our rate of increase in productivity to lag far behind that in countries like Germany and Japan where the savings rate, as a percent of incomes, is several times as high as it is here.

Political finance both causes inflation and requires it in order to make good upon its promises

This political method of mortgaging future productive efforts is inherently less sound and reliable than the funding method employed by responsible financial institutions, but the inherent difficulty is compounded by the practical fact that it is always politically easier to increase the promises than to increase the taxes to make good upon them. By now political organizations throughout the world have made such enormous promises that they cannot possibly keep them in real terms—that is, under conditions of price stability— because the taxes required would constitute a crushing disincentive to productive efforts. However, the attempt to make good on them in nominal terms involves the creation of purchasing power through debt expansion that does not necessarily expand the amount of real goods and services available to be purchased. The tragedy is that the resulting inflation frustrates the expectations not only of the people who are relying upon irresponsible political schemes, but also the expectations of responsible people like our policyholders who are attempting to save out of their current productive efforts in order to provide for their own future needs and responsibilities.

Let me repeat that the habit of saving, and of holding savings in the form of intangible financial claims, was largely formed during the nineteenth century when both the general price level and interest rates declined gently but persistently so that holders of financial claims did extremely well in real terms. However, it is clear that during the last dozen years forgoing consumption in order to accumulate financial claims has become a decreasingly rational thing to do; and the percentage of incomes that is so saved in the United States is diminishing rapidly.

Pay-as-you-go financing doesn't work very well

By now most young people are aware that they are quite unlikely to get as much out of the Social Security system in real terms as they will put into it because the lack of a proper reserve basis for funding the system means that the Social Security taxes that they are paying out of their current incomes are being used to provide current benefits for the presently retired and unproductive people, instead of being invested in productive facilities in order to provide additional real goods and services out of which future real benefits could be provided for them. Thus the Social Security system represents in effect a return to the ancient agrarian approach of supporting the aged and unproductive people through the efforts of the productive young rather than out of the earnings upon the elders' invested savings. This system never worked as well as the modern system of investing savings out of earned incomes in claims, to future goods and services, that in turn finance the real investment that will facilitate the production of those goods and services. In the future it will work even less well than it did in the past, for two reasons. The first is that improved medical care and the fall in the birth rate are producing a rapid increase in the average age of the population in this country so that the burden of providing retirement incomes will also rise rapidly unless productivity increases at a much faster pace than seems likely in view of the current low level of real investment. The other reason is that working hard to support the elderly is incompatible with our current ethics of individualism, which stresses not personal responsibility but personal gratification; so that this system is more likely to produce in the end a revolt of the young than a satisfactory standard of living for the aged. By revolt I do not necessarily mean anything violent, but merely a growing refusal to work hard in order to pay taxes.

Because it does not provide real savings for productive investment

I recently read an analysis of the Social Security system, done by a recognized expert,[1] that takes a more relaxed view of the problem than I do. It points out that to fund the Social Security system the way a life insurance company would do it would require a reserve of roughly $4 trillion, nearly twice the annual Gross National Product of the United States, and asserts that such an enormous sum would have to be invested in Government bonds so that the ability of the Social Security system to meet its obligations would rest upon the ability of the American people to pay taxes, which is what it rests upon now. However, if the Social Security taxes had been used from the start to buy real productive assets, and the benefits had been paid out of the additional production that those assets made possible, the ability of the American people to pay taxes would be much greater than it in fact is, and the growing tendency on the part of productive people to disappear into the subterranean economy would be considerably reduced.

[1] J. W. Van Gorkom, *Social Security 1 and 2, Across the Board,* The Conference Board, March and April 1979.

This point is so crucially important, and is so badly understood by most people, that I would like to restate it another way. In order to fulfill in real terms the promises that the Social Security system is making to the people, without inflation and a crushing burden of taxes, we would have had to save and invest in productive tools and facilities some $4 trillion more than we have in fact saved. If we had made those savings the real standard of living in this country would be higher than it now is, our international competitiveness would not be in question, and the credit of the United States Government would look far more plausible in real terms than it now does.[2]

The process of creating excessive purchasing power, by an expansion of debt at a faster rate than the real economy will respond with the production of additional goods and services, has already proceeded much farther in this country than I would have thought even remotely likely a decade ago. I discussed the hyperinflation in post–World War I Germany in order to emphasize both the identity of the processes at work in Germany then and in the United States now, and the enormous difference in the surrounding circumstances. Starvation is not a threat in America; but by now most of us have seen elderly retired people, who had thought that they had made adequate provision for their needs, in the supermarkets staring at the meat that they can no longer easily afford to buy. That is something that I would not have expected to see in this country during my lifetime. I will return later to some of the other developing indications that the financial system is beginning to break down, but first let us look at the forces that have produced the financial morass into which we are now rapidly sinking.

[2]Mr. Van Gorkom recognizes that the Social Security system has reduced the rate of capital formation in the United States, particularly since the 1977 payroll tax increase. But he does not appear to have grasped the fundamental point that promising future benefits without providing for the investment in productive resources that will enable the promises to be kept in real terms is wrong in principle and mischievous in practice.

SIX

Where We Went Wrong

The question of the causes of inflation can be approached from any number of points of view that result in a corresponding variety of answers. I have tried to point out that mechanically inflation is simply the result of creating purchasing power more rapidly than the output of real goods and services will respond, and for purposes other than investment in productive facilities; and from this point of view there is plenty of blame to go around. I have reviewed the contribution of the private sector's purchasing of inflation hedges with borrowed funds as well as the role of governmental debt formation; and in the next chapter I will assess the consequences as well as the causes of the fall in the external value of the dollar.

Inflation originates in the public sector

However, the record makes it perfectly clear that the initiating cause of inflation is governmental policy, to which the private sector then responds by doing inflationary things of its own. Until recently the main reason why governments pursued inflationary policies was war so that inflation was almost exclusively a wartime and postwar phenomenon; but since World War II inflation has become endemic in peacetime as well. One obvious cause of this new phenomenon is the breaking of the linkage, between the financial system and money with intrinsic value, that began in 1914 and became complete by the beginning of the 1970's. If that is all there is to the story then disaster appears to be inevitable, for it seems altogether improbable that the linkage will be restored, except perhaps in the aftermath of a catastrophic financial collapse. Today there is a fairly large and rapidly growing apocalyptic school that is warning people to prepare themselves for a total financial collapse; and I will make a few practical comments upon their recommendations in Chapter 9.

Fortunately, I believe that there is more to the story than that; and while it is true that endemic inflation could not have occurred without the breaking of the linkage, there are three aspects of modern governmental policy that have contributed greatly to inflation simply by being pushed to an impracticable extreme, and with respect to which a reasonable degree of moderation would reduce the inflationary pressures enormously. The first of these is the attempt to overstabilize or "fine-tune" the economy, the second is the carrying of social democracy to a financially inviable extreme, and the third, in the United States at least, is what I will call the trend toward totalitarian democracy.

The attempt to overstabilize the real economy has inadvertently produced financial instability

This is the point that originally launched me upon this line of reasoning, and so I will start with it. You will recall that in the Introduction I commented that as early as late 1961 it seemed clear to me that the New Economics of the Kennedy Administration was bound to prove financially mischievous because it implied that the burden of debts and of debt service charges relative to incomes would have to rise forever, which is a mathematical impossibility. Well, with the benefit of hindsight it is now obvious that the attempt to use monetary and fiscal policy as controls to keep the economy running stably at the level of full employment and optimum output without inflation has in fact produced endemic and accelerating inflation, wild fluctuations both in the real economy and in financial conditions, and an excessive burden of debts throughout all sectors of the financial system. (The impact of President Johnson's failure to budget responsibly for the war in Vietnam is discussed in the appendix. I will not go into it here because it was an historical accident rather than one of the systematic causes of financial instability with which this book is chiefly concerned.)

Now, the authors of the New Economics were (and are—they're still around) very bright and well-educated people, so it is instructive to inquire how they went so badly wrong. My answers to that question have been scattered throughout this book, but let me try to pull them together here. First, as I pointed out in Chapter 1, ever since the Keynesian revolution in 1936 Economics has been taught in a way that consistently plays down the significance of psychological factors. Second, the academic economists who originated the New Economics were fascinated with the development of mathematical models, and had had insufficient experience in the practical world to realize that one result of the adoption of their policy recommendations would be to create a new motive for economic behavior that would cause a change in relationships that the equations in the model assumed to be unchanging. For example, the savings rate in the United States for many years fluctuated narrowly around an average of 6½ percent of disposable personal income; and so the models assume that it will always be 6½ percent. However, people aren't that stupid. They realize that a rising and now inflation-proofed level of social insurance makes personal saving less necessary, and accelerating inflation makes it foolish. Therefore, the level of inflationary borrowing and spending has considerably exceeded the economists' calculations during the last few years while the savings rate has declined to less than 5 percent of personal disposable incomes.

A practical theory of monetary policy

Finally, the conventional theory of money and credit that I have attempted to refute in detail implies that only money constitutes purchasing power, and that the Central Bank can control the rate at which money is created through its control over bank reserves. There is a relationship between the provision of bank reserves and the overall rate of credit creation, but it is much looser and sloppier than the theory implies; and the practical consequence is that what is called monetary policy is not a fine-tuning control at all. It is a very powerful but very coarse and crude instrument that resembles an off-on switch much more than it does the volume control or water valve that conventional theory visualizes.

In Chapter 2 I tried to give a practical explanation of the rather ambiguous concept of the creation of purchasing power, and to point out that it happened whenever a borrower gained purchasing power but the lender did not believe that he had irretrievably alienated it. The crucial consideration here is liquidity—the ability to turn financial instruments back into ready purchasing power; and while for purposes of theoretical exposition I talked about it in terms of specific loans and the financial instruments that they create, in practice an investment manager thinks about liquidity primarily on a portfolio or institutional basis. As long as he is comfortably confident that he can meet any demands for the withdrawal of funds that are likely to occur he is willing to go on supplying purchasing power by making new loans at what appear to be satisfactory interest rates; but if he starts to worry that withdrawals may be greater than he had anticipated so that he may be caught short of funds, then he begins to want very badly to exchange relatively illiquid financial assets for highly liquid ones. It is essential that we recognize clearly that the factor that controls the rate at which purchasing power gets created is not the money supply but rather the opinion of investment managers about the liquidity of the financial instruments that their institutions hold, relative to the risk that they will be exposed to net withdrawals and the chance that they will be offered better investment opportunities in the reasonably near future.

One of the things that makes investment management such a fascinating business is that we are all constantly trying to outsmart each other with respect to liquidity. If a general shortage of liquidity develops, then the rent that a borrower will have to pay to induce a lender to make a relatively illiquid loan will rise; and anyone who goes into such a period with a surplus of liquidity will get to make some very remunerative investments. On the other hand, once the stringency passes market rates of interest will decline; and anyone who holds on to his liquidity too long may find that he has damaged his investment income, and therefore his ability to pay a competitive return to his own depositors or policyholders, for years to come. Since periods of stringency also threaten to produce net withdrawals from financial institutions, the game can become exceedingly hard on the nerves at times. Whenever such a period threatens to develop an institutional investment manager watches the trend of his withdrawals, as well as his market opportunities, like a hawk.

The importance of being liquid

It is within this context of constant reassessments of liquidity requirements and calculations of the opportunity cost of forgoing investments now versus the possible penalty cost of having to buy liquidity in a tight market (not to mention the possibility of becoming insolvent) that monetary policy becomes crucial. The commercial banks are the last-resort providers of liquidity to the rest of the financial system, and the Central Bank is the institution through which the credit of the National State is mobilized to provide liquidity to the banking system. Contrary to the implications of conventional theory, the Central Bank does not directly control the creation of purchasing power. The financial system as a whole does that. But it does have a great deal of influence upon the liquidity of financial instruments in the marketplace, and therefore upon the willingness of lenders to create additional purchasing power. To take an extreme example, before the Fed-Treasury "accord" of 1951 the American Central Bank pegged the price of 2½ percent Treasury bonds at par. That meant that long-term Treasury bonds were more liquid then than Treasury bills are today, and that every investor who held them could recapture purchasing power at will, with no market risk. The only reason that inflation did not soar in the late 1940's is that practically nobody expected it to do so. Most people expected a depression instead, and so they were very cautious about going into debt in order to create purchasing power. If the Fed pegged the Government bond market today, when everybody does expect inflation, the rate of inflation would go through the roof. In connection with my proposal to banish the word "money" from our technical vocabulary, I also propose to replace the term "monetary policy" with "liquidity policy."

Once inflation becomes endemic the Central Bank is always in a bind, and is constantly under simultaneous attack from both flanks. If it makes available all the liquidity that the market demands, and at a reasonable price, then lenders also make purchasing power readily available by loaning freely, the rate of inflation rises, and the real wealth of people who have been foolish enough to save prudently shrinks while that of people who have been prudent enough to borrow recklessly increases because the nominal value of the things that they have bought goes up and the real burden of their debts falls.

On the other hand, if the Central Bank raises the cost of liquidity (by raising the interest rate at which it will lend to the commercial banks, by increasing the amount of the reserves that the commercial banks must keep on deposit with it, or by selling existing financial assets out of its portfolio into the market in competition with borrowers who are attempting to raise funds by issuing new financial instruments) then interest rates in general will rise and some projects whose expectable rate of return is low will become unfinanceable. If the country has already achieved the full employment of its usable resources then it is highly desirable, from the overall point of view, that some projects be postponed; and as we saw in Chapter 5 one of the functions of the going rate of interest is to determine which projects are worth doing now and which ones should be postponed until interest rates have declined because the economy is less busy. But the particular borrower or promoter whose pet project has been rendered unfinanceable doesn't like it; and he complains to his Congressman who in turn holds a hearing and announces that the Fed is being mean to the home buyer, or the small businessman, or whomever.

Nominal, real and effective interest rates

Once inflation has been around for a while the question whether interest rates are high or low itself becomes a topic for political debate because people begin to think more and more in real terms rather than in nominal terms. Nominal interest rates in the United States today are virtually at historic peaks, but real interest rates are low because the rate of inflation is also historically high. It is important to note that the *effective* rate of interest that determines whether people will want to borrow or not is the nominal interest rate less the *expected* rate of inflation over the life of the loan; and this is both an imprecise and a volatile concept because expectations about the rate of inflation can change rapidly. Moreover, the expectation of a high rate of inflation can produce a very unstable combination of an extremely reasonable effective interest rate, one that stimulates a great demand for borrowings, with an unworkably high nominal rate that makes the satisfaction of that demand exceedingly difficult and dangerous.

The secular trend of inflation in the United States is clearly upward. When I first started thinking about these things in late 1961 prices were stable, and had been for four years. By the beginning of 1969 I was fulminating about the dangers of 3 percent inflation; and by now the rate of inflation has approximately quadrupled. Moreover, there are very few people who expect it to go below 6 percent or so in the foreseeable future, even during a period of recession. Now, an expected average annual rate of inflation of 8 or 9 percent would make a nominal interest rate of 12 or 13 percent appear to be quite reasonable in real terms, and would be very effective in stimulating a very large demand for credit. But the financial system cannot coexist indefinitely with such high nominal interest rates.

Financial institutions borrow short and lend long

As a broad generalization savers want to be able to recapture their purchasing power whenever they need it, and borrowers want to have the use of the borrowed funds as long as they need them. It is one of the functions of financial institutions to accommodate both of them by accepting the risk of borrowing short and lending long. There is always a risk involved in doing that, but before inflation became endemic it was a moderate one; and as we have seen the evolution of the financial markets and of techniques to mobilize the credit of the State in a crisis have reduced it further.

However, once inflation has set in and is expected to continue it ceases to make sense to postpone consumption and save unless nominal interest rates are high enough to suggest that the saver will experience a reasonably satisfactory real return on his savings; and that fact has enormous implications for the survival of our financial system that are currently in the process of unfolding in the real world. One implication that has already caused a great deal of financial turmoil, and is most probably about to cause a great deal more, is the process that is known by the ungainly but accurate name of disintermediation.

The threat of disintermediation

Financial institutions intermediate between savers and borrowers by accepting funds from the one and lending them to the other. Since institutions typically lend for relatively long periods of time, during a period of rising interest rates they cannot raise the yield on their portfolios of loans faster than their old low interest rate loans mature and the funds are reinvested at the new and higher rates, except by selling the old loans on the market at a loss. Now, institutions can take losses without going bankrupt only to the extent of their capital (that is, the amount by which their assets exceed their debts to depositors, policyholders and other creditors); and unfortunately our ideas about the amount of capital that it is reasonable for a financial institution to hold were formed during the nineteenth century when prices and the market for long-term financial assets were more stable and the risk of loss was much smaller than it is today.

For example, mutual life insurance companies that are chartered by the State of New York are limited to holding a maximum of 10 percent of our life insurance liabilities in surplus. All earnings that would cause us to exceed that limit must be paid back to our policyholders as dividends. (At the time that that law was passed, it didn't occur to anybody that a life insurance company would ever write anything except life insurance. Today the fastest growing part of our business is accident and health insurance, against which we are not permitted to hold any surplus at all.) During the nineteenth century 10 percent was enough, but today we are not so sure, so at the Guardian we state our reserves on a very conservative basis and we keep our surplus just as close to the limit as we can; but that makes our Company one of the most strongly capitalized financial institutions in the country.

The Central Bank's dilemma

When market rates of interest rise rapidly it is not possible for financial institutions to raise the yield on their portfolios, or the interest rates that they can afford to pay to their depositors, anywhere near as fast. At some point it makes sense for the individual depositor to withdraw his funds and buy a financial instrument for himself, directly from the market. That is disintermediation. When it becomes severe the Central Bank is faced with the alternatives of seeing the financial institutions that normally provide an efficient mechanism for channeling the country's savings into productive investments melt away, and the bond market collapse under the selling pressure from institutions that are trying to raise the funds to pay off withdrawing depositors (some of whom are not making offsetting purchases from the market but instead are repaying bank loans upon which the interest charges are also soaring), or of providing liquidity to the market to meet the drain. Thus, there is a practical limit to the speed with which nominal interest rates can rise without producing fear, of runaway disintermediation and perhaps even insolvency, that causes financial institutions to cease to be willing to make new loans or to refinance maturing loans. That is what is called a panic or liquidity crisis, and as we have seen the original purpose of central banks was to prevent the occurrence of such disruptive events. However, if the Central Bank pours liquidity into the market at a time when the rate of inflation is high enough to make the effective interest rate a bargain, even more purchasing power will be created by borrowings and the inflation will worsen.

Liquidity policy combats the inflationary overexpansion of credit by driving nominal interest rates up to the point at which disintermediation sets in and causes lenders to become so concerned about their ability to satisfy the increasing demand for withdrawals that they refuse to make new loans or to renew maturing ones. An alternative approach would be for the Central Bank to reduce bank reserves to a level below that which the market demands so that bank credit becomes unavailable at the margin. In either case the level of interest rates is forced up; and while the financially strongest borrowers are accommodated, some of the weaker ones are not. Finally, any of the weaker borrowers who need the funds not to finance a real investment but to refund a maturing debt are driven into bankruptcy.

It is a pretty dilemma indeed. Once inflation has become endemic, it will come to an end only when the financial system becomes too fearful to continue to expand credit at an inflationary rate, but that only happens when the Central Bank creates conditions that are virtually identical to those that it was originally established to prevent. If it fails to scare the financial community sufficiently it does not succeed in breaking the inflation; but on the other hand if it scares it too much it can easily produce a financial crisis or panic that may in turn lead to a depression if the unavailability of credit causes a sufficient number of people and businesses to go broke. Moreover, each time the Central Bank forces the financial system toward disaster and then retreats, the financial community's conviction that it will not be pushed over the edge is reinforced; and the next time the Central Bank has to push it even closer to the brink. We have had three such episodes in the United States since 1966; and so the next one will probably have to be frightening indeed to have much impact upon the rate of inflation. This point has implications for your personal investments that we will also explore in the last chapter.

The financial limits to social democracy

The second major governmental policy that has served as an initiating cause of inflation in the United States (and in a great many other political democracies and some not-so-democratic countries as well) is our growing, and by now financially excessive, commitment to social democracy. It is perfectly feasible[1] for a wealthy and productive country to

---

[1]Whether social democracy is desirable or not is a moral judgment that I will not attempt to make. It seems clear that its practical consequences are by no means entirely benign. Before social democracy arrived, the United States absorbed enormous numbers of immigrants from a wide variety of depressed and/or oppressed lands, many of whom spoke no English and some of whom were illiterate in any language. There were serious transitional problems to be sure, but within a generation or two virtually every such group had been successfully integrated into the American economy. The last great migration was internal—the movement of farm workers forced off the land by the mechanization of agriculture into the cities that provide the highest levels of transfer payments and social services—and it has produced both a human disaster and a social problem of enormous magnitude, the resolution of which is not even remotely in sight. Surely at least part of the reason for these radically different outcomes is that the nineteenth century immigrants had perforce to cope with their new economic environment, and the twentieth century migrants did not.

underwrite a modest standard of living for all of its citizens, without endangering either economic efficiency or price and financial stability, as long as the limits that are inherent in the nature of the enterprise are carefully observed; but unfortunately that has not generally been done.

I almost hate to write this paragraph because the points it makes are so obvious. However, the practical consequences of a mistake are not less severe because it is obvious. First, no society can provide people with a larger income for doing nothing than it is willing to pay for the least valuable work that it wants to get done. Second, no society can provide substantially more in the way of transfer payments (either internally or in foreign aid) in real terms than its people are willing to give up in the form of taxes. It *is* possible to attempt to levy higher taxes than the people will voluntarily pay, but the chief result will be tax evasion and a growing resort to the subterranean economy. It is also possible to attempt to make larger nominal transfer payments than the people are willing to provide in real terms by financing the difference through government borrowing; but the chief result will be inflation.

The subterranean economy

Both of these problems appear to be approaching crisis proportions. I have already covered the impact of inflation upon the financial system, so let us now explore the phenomenon of the subterranean economy. Peter M. Gutmann, Chairman of the Department of Economics and Finance at the Bernard M. Baruch College of the City of New York, introduced this concept in an article in the December 1977 issue of the *Financial Analysts Journal*. He pointed out that as of December 1976 currency in circulation outside banks in the United States amounted to $380.68 per capita—far more than most people who are on payrolls and therefore have to pay withholding taxes normally carry around in their pockets. By comparing the ratio of currency in circulation to checking account balances today with the ratio that prevailed in the pre–World

War II era, before inflation and high taxes had set in, Gutmann arrived at a rough estimate that at least 10 percent of the total economic activity in the United States is being paid for in cash so that it escapes the notice both of the tax collector and of the economic statistician. Since the end of 1976 the currency in circulation outside banks has continued to rise, and by late 1978 it was over $460 per capita. How long has it been since you had $460 in cash in your pocket?

The implications of the subterranean economy concept for national policy are enormous—almost revolutionary. In the first place, it suggests that the official unemployment rate upon which much economic policymaking is based is so wildly overstated that we not only do not have a serious unemployment problem in the United States but in fact the country has been at or close to effective full employment since at least late 1977. (The ex–agricultural workers and their offspring who have been supported by transfer payments for so long that they have become unemployable at the legal minimum wage constitute a separate problem that cannot be solved satisfactorily by macroeconomic policy. The attempt to so solve it has been one of the major causes of the inflationary overexpansion of Federal Government debt.) It also suggests that a large and rapidly rising number of productive people are finding ways of partly or entirely escaping from the burden of income taxation.[2] Finally, it suggests that as long as the current trend of national policy continues we will never see a balanced national government budget again, either in the United States or in most of the other social democracies.

[2]For the sake of formal completeness, it should also be noted that the incidence of *barter* also appears to be rising rapidly in the United States. The bartering of goods is evidently legal, but the exchanging of services may be illegal tax evasion. The fact that the burden of taxation has risen to the point at which people are beginning to avoid it by giving up the conveniences of the system of doing whatever it is that they do best, and exchanging the fruits of their labors for financial instruments that they can then use to buy all the variety of things they want in favor of the cumbersome system of seeking out someone who needs what they can provide, and also can provide what they need, has frightening implications for the efficiency of our economy.

The financial consequences of the trend toward totalitarian democracy

The bulk of this book is about financial trends and developments with respect to which I can claim to speak with some degree of professional authority. However, there is one fundamental trend in our national affairs that, while it is not itself specifically financial, threatens to produce financially ruinous consequences. The United States remains a political democracy, in the sense that in 1980 we will have an opportunity to throw the rascals out of Washington and elect a new set of rascals; but it is also rapidly becoming a totalitarian state in which the politicians constantly pass laws that describe desirable goals in general terms, and delegate to the bureaucracy broad powers to make and enforce regulations that are designed to achieve them. Unfortunately, those laws and regulations are frequently drawn up with little or no consideration of the actual consequences that they will produce in the real world, or whether the goal is really worth the cost that is imposed upon our society in the attempt to accomplish it. The waste, costs and inefficiencies that this trend is producing are more than even a country as wealthy as the United States can bear without losing its international competitiveness and experiencing a decline in its real standard of living. If the United States is to remain a viable society, the burden of government regulation of virtually all aspects of our lives must be substantially reduced; and the regulations that remain must take some account of practical feasibility and real costs.

Examples of regulatory absurdity could easily fill the rest of this book, or a whole library of books, so I will cite just two taken from the field of motor vehicles. For about three years the National Highway Transportation Safety Administration required that new heavy trucks be equipped with a braking system, at a cost of about $1500 per truck, that was so dangerous that truck drivers generally disabled it at the first opportunity. Again, the Federal antipollution regulations have caused the cars that have been produced in this country since 1972 to start so badly and run so poorly that many of their owners disable the expensive antipollution equipment in the attempt to achieve satisfactory performance, or burn less expensive leaded gas that disables the catalytic exhaust converter—after which they produce enormously more pollutants than the pre-1972 cars did. The automobile industry has spent huge sums to meet the Federally mandated pollution and mileage standards; and now the bureaucrats are talking about a new set of standards to become effective after 1985 that would require a radically different engine technology—before the industry has been able to amortize the investments it has made to meet the current standards.

I said earlier that the chief cause of the inflationary bias our economy has developed is the fact that progressively more and more of the purchasing power that is created by credit expansion is going to finance consumption while less and less is being used for productive real investment. A further problem is that a great deal of the real investment that is being made is going into environmental and other frills rather than into directly productive facilities. It is certainly reasonable to use part of our late twentieth century wealth to clean up some of the mess that we made in the nineteenth and earlier twentieth centuries in the process of becoming wealthy; but not to the extent of damaging our productivity, international competitiveness or solvency. It would also be a good idea to pay some attention to the wishes of the people who are going to have to pay for all the good that the Government is doing us. Certainly most American automobile owners would not have agreed to the imposition of the pollution and mileage standards if they had realized what it was going to cost them, not only in the price but in grief and aggravation. Personally, I was fortunate that the nature of my work gave me some inkling of what was about to happen; and when the excise tax was removed in 1971 I promptly bought one of the last satisfactory cars that was made in this country. Since then I have maintained it with tender loving care in the hope that I never have to buy another one.

Political mandates versus the market economy

Political mandates and subsidies also disrupt the process by which the marketplace decides which investments are worth making and which ones will not provide a sufficient increase in human productivity or satisfaction to justify the cost. For example, in 1978 the Guardian lent a water company $8 million of the $13 million cost of building a mechanical filtration plant at one of its reservoirs, and the expense of repaying us will increase the cost of the water to the consumers by about 30 percent. Now, that reservoir has been in use since 1905 and the people in its service area have been drinking the water without noticeable complaint for three quarters of a century. The filtration system will reduce the turbidity of the water to an extent that may be visible to the naked eye, and it does provide an extra margin of safety if something should start to go wrong with the reservoir; but I do not know of anyone in the Company or the service area who believes that those benefits are worth a 30 percent rate increase. However, since the plant was politically mandated the opinions of the people involved are not relevant. The Company's Chief Engineer tells me that they may be required to filter all their water supplies. That would cost another $35 million to $40 million, which is more than half of its present plant account; and the large increase in the Company's debt service requirements that would result from making this enormous investment at the current high level of interest rates would cause the price of the water to the customers to double. We will lend to an obviously creditworthy borrower regardless of whether or not we think that the project being financed makes sense, but the Company would not voluntarily make such investments unless its management and Board of Directors believed that they were sufficiently necessary or desirable to justify the cost.

The costs of politically and bureaucratically mandated investments, and of sheer idiocies like building power dams and then not closing them because they might drown a species of minnow that nobody had ever noticed before the dam was started,[3] or wipe out a species of lousewort that nobody but a botanist can tell from all the other louseworts,[4] are more than even the United States can bear without a decline in our national standard of living; and the financing of ill-considered or totally useless investments gives an extra fillip to the inflationary creation of excessive credit that is completely unnecessary. The Federal Government has set up a Committee to second-guess the bureaucrats with respect to the most obvious idiocies; but the system of political mandates will continue to subvert the principle by which the market system of economic organization assures that the best and most practical decisions that are available usually get made.

Why the market system does things better than the political system

That principle is that the people who are most intimately connected with a given problem have a major incentive to find the right solution; and if they find that they have started off in the wrong direction to stop and start over as soon as that fact becomes clear. Consider the likelihood that a bureaucrat sitting in Washington would guess correctly what young women are going to want to wear next spring. Fortunately, on Seventh Avenue in New York City we have thousands of entrepreneurs with experience in that business, and a major financial stake in coming up with the right answer. Being human, they make mistakes; but if they find that they are making skirts when the girls want jeans, they stop, sell

[3] I am aware that the Tellico dam, the one that might do in the Tennessee Snail Darter, may not be closed for the very practical reason that the 25,000 acres of land it would inundate may turn out to be capable of producing food with a greater value than the electricity that the dam would generate. It is to be noted that the dam was built by the Tennessee Valley Authority, which is a Federal bureaucracy, not by a private profit motivated utility company.

[4] Bureaucrats are unlikely to worry about the saver and investor, but as I mentioned in the preface, today he also is becoming an endangered species.

the skirts for whatever they will bring and promptly start making pants so that the cost of the mistake is minimized.

Collectivists frequently argue that the great size and complexity of modern economies require central planning and control. The truth is precisely the other way around. The more complex an economy becomes the more necessary it becomes that decisions be made by experienced businessmen who know their markets and who have a personal interest in getting the decisions right if it is to produce the goods and services that the people want enough to pay for voluntarily, and at a cost that they can afford. It takes a bureaucrat to build a Tellico dam, and a Khrushchev to plow up millions of acres of land where there is not enough rainfall to grow wheat. The market system of organization makes mistakes self-correcting at the minimum cost, but the political system of organization frequently produces colossal and costly blunders when it attempts to make economic and financial decisions.

A remarkable illustration of this point is to be found in the book *A Time for Truth*,[5] written by the ex-Secretary of the Treasury, William E. Simon. I had known Bill at Salomon Brothers and considered him to be a sensible, levelheaded man; and so I was completely baffled by the chaos that the Federal Energy Office, of which he was the Czar, created in the attempt to keep the price of petroleum products below the level at which supply and demand would have balanced each other in the marketplace. Bill discovered by his own experiences in Washington that it is impossible in practice for politicians and bureaucrats to overrule the market without making a complete botch of things. Since he left Washington he has been studying John Locke, Adam Smith and the other great men who first worked out the principles of the nineteenth century liberal system of limited government, maximum individual freedom and reliance upon the market to provide the goods and services that people want enough

---

[5]William E. Simon, *A Time for Truth*, Readers Digest Press, McGraw-Hill, New York, 1978.

to pay for; and he has come to realize that it is wrong in principle as well as impossible in practice to overrule the market. This double-barreled approach, in terms of practical experience as well as sound theory, has resulted in an extremely clear and convincing book. I strongly recommend it to all thoughtful Americans. We once knew that an economy and society will work better when it has no Czars, or even Khans, and I hope that we rediscover that fact before our financial system and productive economy are irreparably damaged.

SEVEN

The Collapse of the International Financial System

The social value of the international financial system

The main reason why a stable and reliable international financial system is necessary is that there are many countries whose citizens do not trust their domestic financial system sufficiently to be willing to hold their wealth in the form of intangible financial claims that are denominated in the local currency. They either want to hold it in the form of real tangible things, or in financial claims denominated in the currency of a country that they do trust. Untrustworthy countries existed in the nineteenth century, they became more numerous after the link between financial systems and money with intrinsic value was broken during World War I, and their number soared after World War II when decolonization created a multitude of politically weak states whose economic viability is doubtful.

There are only three ways that the real investments that increase human productivity, thereby raising the standard of living, can be financed in such countries. Other countries may be willing to give them real goods or services outright, for military, political or humanitarian reasons. Or they may be able to borrow from countries whose citizens do trust their financial institutions. To the extent that neither of these is possible the only alternative remaining is for the Government to finance real investment itself by creating purchasing power out of thin air by deficit financing, with the private sector being forced to part with the corresponding real resources by the hidden tax of inflation. (Of course, it is also possible for the Government to commandeer real goods or services by naked military force. But in all except the most abysmally run countries the same end is accomplished a little more gracefully by inflation.) One of the saddest facts about postwar economic development is that most of the new developing countries have elected to finance development through inflation rather than by establishing a stable financial system that would encourage private savings and investment. Thus for many years they have been saddled with the waste and inefficiencies of the political system of making investment decisions, as compared with the efficiency and flexibility of the market system, that we in the United States are now saddling upon ourselves; and also with rates of inflation that make personal saving fruitless.

Key currencies in classical antiquity

As long as money with intrinsic value prevailed, all that was required to run a successful key currency system was for the principal banking nation to avoid debasing its coinage. For example, in the fifth century B.C. Athens was the most important commercial, maritime and banking center in the world. Her coins—the Athenian silver owls—were freely accepted throughout the Mediterranean world and served as a recognized standard of value for 600 years, even though Athens itself was conquered by the Spartans and then by the Macedonians and eventually declined to the status of a hick college town for upper-class Romans. The reason for the success of this earliest key currency was that in spite of all their wars and tribulations, the Athenians never gave in to the temptation to increase the purchasing power of their silver by alloying it and thus debasing the coinage.

The Romans were not so wise. The Roman Empire was openly based upon military power and conquest, and the primary sources of Roman wealth were first plunder, and then taxes and tribute exacted from the provinces. The Romans spent this money freely on real goods and services imported from the provinces so that, in our modern terms, they had a steadily very large negative balance of trade—in fact, throughout the imperial period Italy had to import food to survive. This system worked fine as long as there were new lands to plunder of their precious metals; but even before the fall of the Republic, in the intervals between fresh conquests, the Roman economy showed the symptoms of key currency crises similar to those in the United Kingdom during the nineteenth century. Money drained out of Rome to pay for African wheat and Eastern luxuries, interest rates rose to crisis levels, the provinces were not permitted to borrow in Rome and Romans were required to invest their money only in Italy. During these periods the coinage was frequently debased, and the provinces were forced to pay their taxes in gold and silver bullion while they had to accept the alloyed Roman coins at their previous metallic value in payment for exports to Rome. Obviously, this system only worked as long as there were Roman legions around to make it work.

In the years after Caesar Augustus it began to work less well because the moral and physical fibre of the Roman people was deteriorating. During the Republic Rome had been a nation of sturdy farmers and well-disciplined soldiers believing firmly in a religion that preached the patriotic and martial virtues. It was a place you had to respect even though you wouldn't want to live there. The rot set in with the unheard-of idea of actually paying the soldiers, and from then on it was straight downhill to the imperial welfare state of the Caesars. The sturdy paganism of the Republic gave way to a thousand debilitating religions from the East and the practice of a thousand vices from all over the Empire. The birth rate declined as the Romans decided to have fun, not children, so that the legions had increasingly to be filled up with expensive and unreliable mercenaries. This moral decay was reflected in the declining metallic value of the Roman coinage. At the beginning of the imperial period Caesar Augustus brought the treasure of Egypt to Rome and purified the coinage, but Nero diluted the silver denarius by 10 percent. By 260 A.D. the silver content of the denarius was down to 5 percent, and the Roman Empire was well on its way to collapse.

It is easy to condemn the Roman Empire as brutally exploitative, which it was; but we must also remember that the Pax Romana gave the civilized world the longest period of uninterrupted peace, prosperity and progress that it has ever known. When it collapsed civilization also disappeared in Western Europe for half a millennium. The Roman denarius served as a satisfactory international medium of exchange for two centuries, and it had a better record of maintaining its value over the years than most modern currencies.

An early experiment with price and wage controls

One final note before we move on to modern times. In the twilight of the Roman Empire the Emperor Diocletian imposed comprehensive price and wage controls. The resulting shortages and inefficiencies caused widespread suffering and riots. Diocletian had to relax the controls considerably in the original Phase III, and the next Emperor—Constantine— abolished them altogether. There are two morals to this story. The first is that there is no situation so bad that controls will not make it worse, and the second is that no power on earth—not even the Roman Emperor—can reconcile controls and economic efficiency. Really effective price and wage controls can only be maintained through naked force—as in the immediate postwar occupation of Germany or in the Soviet Union today—and then only at the cost of depressing the real standard of living. Inflation is bad enough, but a financial inflation disguised by price and wage controls is worse.

Now let's move along a couple of millennia. Nothing much happened that is relevant to the development of international financial systems between the reign of Diocletian and the Battle of Waterloo *except* the evolution of the financial system of intangible claims, which we reviewed in Chapter 3. The development of structured financial systems has created two new problems that did not exist, or at least were far less important, in classical antiquity. First, inflation is much easier to accomplish now than it was then. When Nero wanted to inflate he had to call in all the currency, melt it down, alloy it and recoin it all over again. Today the Open Market Committee of the Federal Reserve System accomplishes the same result by murmuring a ritual formula instructing the Federal Reserve Bank of New York to buy some Treasury bills.

The necessary conditions for a key currency system

Second, the conditions that lead the people of one nation to honor the currency of another nation, and even accumulate balances in it, get considerably more complicated. Mediterranean traders accepted the Athenian owl because it was intrinsically valuable, and the Roman provinces accepted the alloyed denarius because the legions made them take it. But why would a nineteenth century Argentinian rancher keep his spare money in a sterling deposit in London, or a twentieth century Italian hold a dollar balance in New York? He will do so only if two interrelated requirements are met. First, he wants to earn a reasonably satisfactory rate of interest on his savings and, second, he wants to be reasonably confident that the real value of his savings will be maintained at least as well as is likely in any of the other currencies available to him that provide a similarly attractive rate of interest. Obviously, a higher rate of interest can compensate for a higher rate of inflation since what really counts is the comparison of the real rate of return available from alternative investments denominated in the various currencies. If the expectable real rate of return from deposits in all available currencies appears to be negative, there will be a run from money into precious metals, real estate and other real goods. Today many people do fear that the real rate of return from all paper currencies will be negative; and in the United States, along with many other countries, the fear is justified. That is why the price of gold has gone through the roof, and borrowing in order to buy inflation hedges is increasing rapidly.

The conditions under which a country's currency will inspire confidence in foreigners appear to me to be the following: First, sufficient military strength and political stability to make defeat or revolution appear unlikely. Second, sufficient wealth and economic progress to make it appear likely that the key currency country will be able to meet its obligations on schedule. Third, a record of honorable dealings with foreigners that suggests that it will be willing to honor its obligations. Fourth, a demonstrated interest in maintaining both the internal and the external value of its money. These are pretty stiff conditions, and most currencies do not satisfy them very well most of the time. When one currency does meet them satisfactorily for an extended period of time, it becomes generally used in international trade and finance and thus becomes a key currency.

The United Kingdom and the pound sterling

During the entire century between the end of the Napoleonic Wars in 1815 and the beginning of World War I in 1914 the record of the United Kingdom on each of these counts was superb. The British constitutional monarchy was clearly the most stable government in the world. The Royal Navy was so obviously the strongest in the world that throughout the entire period nobody was foolish enough to challenge it. The British Army was fighting somebody somewhere on the fringes of the Empire almost constantly, but the wars were small and short, comfortably remote from the British Isles, and anyway the British always won. The period was one of rapid economic progress and accumulating wealth in the United Kingdom. The standards of British finance and of the City of London were the highest in the world. After the Napoleonic Wars commodity prices fell steadily throughout the rest of the nineteenth century so that the real value of the pound sterling roughly doubled during the century, and did even better than that as measured from the peak of the wartime inflation in 1814. Since the real value of money was rising interest rates declined substantially, producing large profits for holders of long-term British government bonds. As far as the external value of the pound was concerned, there were several crises and runs during the nineteenth century and each time interest rates were deliberately raised sharply, at the cost of a temporary depression in the United Kingdom, until the run subsided. Throughout the century the United Kingdom was an island of prosperity, stability and commercial honor in an otherwise insecure and revolutionary world.

Even in its decline the sterling system had a touch of nobility. The liquidation of foreign assets and inflation during World War I left the pound not really worth its prewar parity of $4.86 U.S., but the British had a curious notion that debts should be discharged at 20 shillings in the pound and for half a dozen years they deliberately sacrificed the domestic economy to the goal of getting the pound back to the prewar parity and keeping it there; until the financial crisis of the early 1930's made it impossible. In September 1931 they let the pound float, and the international monetary system of fixed exchange rates collapsed. World trade shrank as it became difficult to make payments or get financing, and the crisis of the early thirties developed into the Great Depression.

The foundations of the dollar standard

After World War II the United States dollar was the obvious candidate for the role of the key currency in the postwar international monetary system. The United States was clearly the dominant military power in the world. The political strains and divisions of the Depression years had been overcome by the need for unity during wartime so that our domestic political structure was extremely stable. The United States was not only the wealthiest country in the world, it also had the only large industrial economy that had not been devastated by the war and, in addition, we had the fantastic fertility of the Middle West to feed an impoverished and starving world. During most of the postwar era we lent freely on generous terms and even gave away substantial sums to help finance the postwar economic reconstruction both of our allies and of our recent enemies. It was an act of unprecedented generosity, and clearly most of the world owed the United States an enormous debt of gratitude. It is no wonder that the theory of the dollar gap—a permanent demand for dollars to finance net exports from the United States—lingered on until long after the United States had, in fact, lapsed into a permanent balance of payments deficit.

The fatal flaw in the key currency system

I believe that any key currency system based on a credit or paper money has an inherent tendency toward self-destruction that will eventually bring it down unless something else comes along to sweep the system away before it develops to its logical conclusion. Let me try to make this point first by theoretical reasoning and then I will illustrate its application in the case of the dollar, for this is the first time in history that an international monetary system based upon a credit currency did survive to its logically inevitable conclusion.

A key currency is by definition a currency that the people of other countries accept without question, and in which they seek to invest their surplus wealth in the form of deposits and securities. *This means that the people of the key currency country can raise their own standard of living and enjoy more goods and services than they produce simply by running a balance of payments deficit and creating enough of their own money to pay for it.* They can also use it to buy investment assets abroad without having to give up any tangible goods or services in exchange. The motives of the American people were much more praiseworthy than were the Romans', but the practical effect of the balance of payments deficit was exactly the same in both cases—to raise the standard of living in the key currency country by buying goods and services and investment assets on balance from the rest of the world in exchange for money. The only major difference was that since the Romans had a limited metallic currency they eventually ran out of money and then they either had to get it back by taxing the provinces, or go out and conquer a new country with a fresh hoard of treasure. In the United States, with a paper credit currency, we could go on spending and investing more than we produced indefinitely, as long as foreigners believed that they could in the end turn their rising dollar balances back into real goods and services at something like the current price level.

I know that many people believe that it is better to run a balance of payments surplus and to sell more abroad than you buy there, but there is a monetary illusion here that is sometimes very hard to see through. Think about the matter in real terms for a moment and forget all about money. Then it must be clear that what raises the real standard of living in the country is *imports* not exports. Happiness is driving a German Mercedes, not working hard to produce Cadillacs to ship to the Germans. Increasing net exports raises *money* incomes at home, and under conditions of unemployment it will increase total real output and incomes through the multiplier effect; but it also means that the surplus country is producing and selling to foreigners more real goods and services than it is getting back from them, and balancing the books by accumulating a hoard of their money. Assuming a condition of more or less full employment, the real standard of living will necessarily be higher if a country is a net importer rather than a net exporter. The Germans and the Japanese haven't waked up to this fact yet, but I imagine that they will in time.

The collapse of the dollar standard

During the early postwar period, with the tremendous worldwide demands for American goods, nobody considered an increase in his dollar balance to be a problem; but over the decades the balances rose steadily. As late as 1959 the foreign dollar balances were about the same size as our gold reserves so that externally the dollar still appeared to be almost literally as good as gold—even better, because you can earn interest on dollars while you have to pay somebody to keep an eye on your gold. But over the next decade we spent and invested abroad about $20 billion more than we earned from and sold to the rest of the world. The trend was worrisome but the figures were not yet of an alarming size and, while foresighted people warned that the trend could not go on indefinitely, there seemed to be plenty of time. Then came the manic year 1968 when optimism ran riot and businessmen in the United States were borrowing billions to finance mergers and acquisitions. That was followed by the money crunch of 1969–1970. Federal Reserve policy aimed at squeezing the banking system remorselessly and making credit very scarce and expensive until inflation was killed off. Apparently the Fed simply did not understand that the banks could partially evade the squeeze by borrowing Eurodollars from their foreign branches to lend to their customers in the United States.

In 1968 and 1969 the banks increased their Eurodollar borrowings by $10 billion and the total short-term liabilities of the United States also rose about $10 billion to around $46 billion, against which we held official reserves of foreign exchange and gold amounting to about $17 billion. Since the United States was also running a substantial balance of payments deficit, this was a situation in which foreign holders of dollar balances were bound to begin to wonder if it was still possible to turn them back into real goods and services at anything like the current prices. The situation had now become quite unstable, and we could have avoided a run on the dollar only by pursuing responsible domestic policies that were seen to be designed to preserve the external value of the dollar. What actually happened was radically different. After the failure of the Penn Central Railroad Fed policy swung abruptly to aggressive ease in order to halt the developing panic in the securities markets. From that moment on a run on the dollar was just about inevitable.

During 1971 the dollar balances of the foreign central banks rose $20 billion as people rushed to borrow dollars in New York and exchange them into other currencies at the fixed rates that then prevailed. Those fixed rates could only be maintained by the foreign central banks issuing unlimited amounts of their own currencies in exchange for the flood of dollars. This had two consequences. The first was that as long as the exchange rates were fixed the central banks could not control inflation in their own countries. They had to issue all the marks, yen or francs that the market demanded, and the money was then lent at interest within their borders. Second, unless the American authorities were willing to tighten credit in the United States—which they weren't—the attempt to peg the dollar was bound to fail eventually because the potential supply of borrowable dollars was literally infinite. The foreign central banks were certain to lose money in the end, and the longer they held the rate the more they would lose. The only possible way to shut off the flood of dollars was to go to floating rates and let the market put the price on the dollar that it thought was right. The sensible thing would have been to go to floating rates as soon as the run developed. Instead the central banks made one last stab at maintaining fixed rates based on a devalued dollar with the result that the speculation continued. In 1973 the foreign central banks finally gave up the attempt to maintain fixed exchange rates against the dollar. However, they are not yet ready to let the market set the rate in spite of the fact that the creditworthiness of the United States is still declining; and so the borrowing and shorting of dollars continues.[1]

Summary analysis of the collapse of the system of fixed foreign exchange rates

The important points about the dollar crisis of 1971–1973 are first, that the international acceptability of the dollar in the post–World War II era was based upon the predominant military, economic and financial power of the United States, and upon the prestige that that predominant position commanded, and upon the debt of gratitude that the United States had earned by the generous and constructive role it played during the period of postwar political and economic reconstruction. The second point is that the unquestioned international acceptablility of the dollar meant that the United States could raise its domestic standard of living by being a net buyer of real goods and services and investment assets from the rest of the world in exchange for increasingly overvalued dollars. Third, the resulting steady growth of the dollar balances slowly but inevitably destroyed confidence in the dollar, leading first to the run and devaluation in 1971 and then to the complete breakdown of the fixed-rate international monetary system at the beginning of 1973.

The record since 1973

In the years since 1973 several additional things have gone wrong that have further weakened confidence in the creditworthiness of the United States. First, the oil embargo that

---

[1]From this point on I will stop bothering you with numbers because in the realm of international finance they are coming to resemble the numbers that prevailed during the German hyperinflation. During the last years of the hyperinflation a large German bank added two stories to its building, and when the Managing Director was asked what they were for, he replied, "To store all the zeroes." When you talk about the American balance of payments deficit or the accumulated external liabilities of the United States today, you need a plentiful supply of zeroes.

accompanied the Arab-Israeli war late that year and the subsequent enormous increase in the world price of petroleum—things that nobody would have believed that the United States would have tolerated before the withdrawal from Vietnam made it clear that it would not be politically feasible to do anything effective about them—should have made it as obvious to American politicians as it was to our foreign creditors that our political and military prestige had fallen well below the danger point. Second, in 1973 the inflation rate in the United States was one of the lowest among the major developed nations. Today it is one of the highest, and that has further weakened our creditworthiness. Third, since 1977 the United States has been running a spectacular balance of trade deficit.

There are two basic reasons for the trade deficit. First, the United States is the only major nation in the world that has made no serious attempt to adjust to the new level of oil prices. The bureaucrats have been rushing around making life as complicated as possible for everyone else; and it may be that in the future utility and industrial boilers will have to be made by the Tinkertoy Company so that their burners can be changed as often as Mr. Schlesinger changes his mind about the fuel that ought to be burned in them. However, it has not yet proved to be politically feasible to accept the moderate decline in our national standard of living that would result from importing no more petroleum than we can pay for out of earnings.

The second basic reason for the trade deficit will be covered in more detail in Chapter 8. The portion of our incomes that we save and invest in real productive assets has shrunk so much that the rate at which the productivity of our labors is rising has fallen to a small fraction of that in the hard currency countries where savings as a percent of incomes are several times as large as they are here, with the result that the United States is becoming uncompetitive in world markets.

Finally the policy of "benign neglect" of the external value of the dollar continued, for all practical purposes, until

November 1, 1978; and it constituted just about the most egregious example of beggar-my-neighbor trade policy on record. By now the United States has cashed in on all the good will that we had earned during the preceding quarter century of generous and responsible external policies; and today it would be absurd to say that most other nations owe us anything. The strong currency countries have lost export markets and domestic jobs because of the depreciation of the dollar, and they have been forced to issue excessive amounts of their own financial instruments in exchange for the enormous outpouring of dollar-denominated debt instruments to keep them from depressing the external value of the dollar further and giving the United States an even greater trade advantage.

By the end of October 1978 the floating dollar was sinking like a stone, and the American securities markets were visibly headed for a panic. At long last, the policy of benign neglect had to go. On November 1, the rediscount rate (the rate at which the Federal Reserve Banks will lend to the commercial banks—in most other countries it would be called the bank rate) was raised by 1 percentage point to a record 9½ percent; and lines of credit totaling the equivalent of $30 billion, which can be used to buy dollars on the foreign exchange market, were arranged. If anyone had asked me, I would have recommended that the rediscount rate be raised immediately by 3 or 4 percentage points. In a crisis you want to do something that the market finds to be shocking, and absolutely convincing. You may recall that the last time there was a run on the pound sterling interest rates on British Government bonds went to 17 percent, a new high by several percentage points; and the market was convinced.

The $30 billion kitty appears to be based upon a fallacy that central bankers and politicians evidently cannot disabuse themselves of. Every time a run on a currency develops calculations are made about the largest sum that could possibly be thrown at the exchange; and the market then proceeds to confound the experts by throwing several times that amount at it. The Authorities seem to believe that there is a fund of dollars out there that foreigners have received as a result of our balance of payments deficit, and that once we have bought or borrowed them all back the problem is solved. In fact, of course, most of the dollars were borrowed for the express purpose of selling them short; or were generated by leads and lags in making commercial payments, which amounts to the same thing. As long as people believe that the currency will continue to depreciate, and as long as credit remains readily available in the country whose currency is under attack, the amount that can be thrown at the market is quite literally infinite. In the twelve months to the end of October 1978 the dollar had fallen about 30 percent on average against the strong currencies; and when a speculator or hedger is winning to the extent of 30 percent per annum, on funds that are virtually all borrowed so that the profit on his equity is several hundred percent, there is no feasible interest rate that he will not be willing to pay and no feasible kitty that he and his fellow speculators and hedgers cannot overwhelm. The only sure way to beat off such an attack is to take a leaf from the book of Dr. Schacht and make credit marginally unavailable in the domestic market. Unless that is done, the dollar will remain vulnerable until our balance of payments has improved dramatically and, more specifically, until our dependence upon oil imported from the dangerously unstable Middle East has been corrected.

A key currency country is a financial institution, and should behave like one

Politicians and social democrats often ask plaintively why the United States must now accept external discipline and act with financial responsibility instead of continuing to conduct our affairs to suit our domestic convenience. The answer is that a key currency country is in effect a financial institution for the rest of the world that accepts deposits from people who do not trust their national financial systems, and in turn makes development loans to countries in which the funds cannot be raised on the domestic market. In the process the key currency country, like any other financial institution, borrows short and lends long. As long as its creditworthiness is unquestioned this poses no problems, and it can be quite profitable. But, in order to remain creditworthy a financial institution must act in a way that inspires confidence in its creditors. The United States has not done that—in fact, since the early 1960's it has done almost exactly the opposite. The consequence is that we now are stuck with an intractable problem of the dollar balances that most of our creditors would really rather hold in a more reliable currency, just as the United Kingdom after 1931 was stuck with the problem of the sterling balances. In these circumstances, a continuation of financially irresponsible behavior involves an unacceptably large risk that the American standard of living will be substantially depressed by the increasing domestic cost of our imports and the decreasing external value of our exports that would result from a continuing slide in the foreign exchange value of the dollar.

EIGHT

What Can Be Done About It? Recommendations for National Policy

The road to financial disaster

In Chapters 2 through 7 I tried to tell you how our financial system really works in practice, what it accomplishes when it is working well, and also why it isn't working very well any more. I discussed a variety of political trends, some of which began nearly half a century ago and all of which have accelerated rapidly since 1961, that have on balance enormously increased the demand for the unearned purchasing power that is created both by subsidies and other transfer payments and by the extension of credit, at the same time that they have decreased the incentive to earn additional income by working to increase the supply of real goods and services that are available to be purchased. During and after 1976, those trends have also caused the personal savings rate in the United States to decline sharply.

This divergence, between a falling rate of real savings and a rising demand for unearned purchasing power, has created a gap that cannot be filled in real terms because the only possible source of unearned real purchasing power is real savings. So the gap between the lowered level of real savings that people are willing to make by forgoing consumption and the increased purchasing power that people demand, and that today it is deemed politically advisable to provide, is filled in nominal terms by creating the additional purchasing power out of thin air by means of an expansion of the amount of credit outstanding. The inevitable result is inflation.

The inflationary process has already caused a number of highly undesirable results, both in the United States and elsewhere; and the rate at which things are going wrong is accelerating. Nominal interest rates are at levels that threaten the financial system with disintermediation, but the personal savings rate is not recovering because the expectable real interest rate is zero at best, and probably is negative.[1] In the late twentieth century people who save and hold their wealth in the form of the intangible claims that finance productive real investment do not end up with more purchasing power than they had saved because they received a real rent for the use of their savings, as they did in the nineteenth century. Today they are likely to find that they get back less real purchasing power than they had saved and invested; and the growing realization that during an inflation forgoing consumption in order to save is a mug's game has depressed the savings rate in the United States to a disastrously low level. As recently as 1975 the American people saved 7.7 percent of their personal disposable incomes, but by the end of 1978 the savings rate had dropped to less than 5 percent.

The correspondingly low level of real investment that the decline in the savings rate has caused, in combination with the fact that an increasing portion of the real investments that we do make is going into nice but unproductive environmental frills is also producing a disastrous drop in the

---

[1]Bear in mind the impact of the income tax upon both the demand for, and the supply of, credit. Interest earned, except that upon municipal bonds, is taxable; and interest paid is tax deductible. When this factor is taken into consideration, it is clear that the real rates of interest earned and paid are both negative for most people and businesses. It is no wonder that there is a great demand to borrow, and a growing disinclination to save.

rate at which our national economic productivity is improving. It has already fallen far below the rate that is being achieved by the strong currency countries, whose governments do most of the same inflationary things that our Government does but whose people save and invest a much larger part of their incomes than we do. The pre-1971 overvaluation of the dollar that resulted from the great confidence that the rest of the world had in the United States, and that in turn caused a higher standard of living here than we were earning by our own productive efforts, ended long ago; and the dollar now appears to be decidedly undervalued against the strong currencies in terms of current transactions.

Nevertheless confidence in the foreign exchange value of the dollar has not returned; and it is unlikely to do so in the foreseeable future, for two reasons. The first is that the high rate of inflation and the low rate of productivity gain in the United States, as compared with the strong currency countries, suggest that in the long run the dollar is a sinking ship no matter how cheap it is at the moment; and the second is our long-standing failure to take any effective steps to reduce our dependence upon imported oil or to reduce the steady increase in our foreign indebtedness that oil imports, coming on top of a continuing deterioration in most of the other components of our balance of payments, have produced. It has not yet proved to be politically feasible to accept the moderate fall in our national standard of living that importing only the oil that we can afford without additional borrowings would entail, even though the continuing accumulation of dollar balances in foreign hands and the erosion of confidence in the United States threaten to cause a disastrous fall in our real standard of living as the consequence of an indefinitely prolonged slide in the external value of the dollar.

The American people are no longer saving enough to preserve the international competitiveness of our economy; and if present trends continue we are likely to reduce our savings rate progressively further for the simple but sufficient reason that saving no longer makes sense. In that case we will also see the progressive substitution of Federal Government financing, for that which the private sector used to provide, as the only way that is left to accomplish whatever level of real investment that it remains possible to accomplish. And, since the Federal Government does not save, the real resources will be made available for investment by a progressive increase in the hidden tax of inflation, thereby accomplishing a further reduction in the incentive to save.

As a practical matter, we may be rescued from the consequences of a further collapse in the external value of the dollar in spite of ourselves by the growing political instability and violence in much of the rest of the world that decolonization, the Cold War and the failure of first British and then American international leadership have produced. The appendix will point out that that is what happened in 1968, and the United States remains one of the safest havens for wealth in an increasingly unsafe world. I will cover some of the implications of that for your own investments in the next chapter.

The next localized disaster

The inflationary overexpansion of Government debt is already well advanced in the United States with respect to housing. Federal Agencies now provide about a quarter of the total mortgage loans on houses and farms, and they lend the credit of the Government through guarantees to facilitate the financing of a good deal of the rest. And this, in conjunction with a specific example of totalitarian democracy called the Equal Credit Opportunity Act, contains the seeds of a real disaster. Ideological attitudes being what they are in the United States today, let me quote the normally restrained *London Economist* on this one:

> America's Equal Credit Opportunity Act makes it illegal for housing loans to be refused on grounds of race, color, religion, national origin, sex, marital status or age. Since the only reason why some loans ever used to be refused was that they were

uneconomic, but since everybody who is refused a loan can now say that this is because of illegal discrimination against her or him, the crazy consequence has been to multiply uneconomic housing loans and send house prices through the roof. The worst sort of reflation is one that dissipates itself instantly into real estate inflation and America (now that married couples' incomes have to be aggregated in ratings for housing loans) is the first country to have deliberately created that bubble in pursuit of antisexist reform. (June 24, 1978)

I am afraid that the damage has already been done with respect to houses. It seems altogether probable that we will have a period of extreme financial stringency at some time in the near future regardless of whether the financial authorities want it or not; and so much mortgage debt has been incurred in the process of pushing up the prices of houses that the next crunch is virtually certain to depress them substantially. The impact upon the net worth of a great many American families, and upon the confidence with which they view the future and consequently their willingness to spend on consumption, is likely to be severe. Thus the Federal Government, by pursuing general policies that produced an endemic inflation that has finally caused most Americans to become inflation hedgers, by a specific act of totalitarian democracy that has permitted a number of American families to borrow more than the financial system would have lent them voluntarily, and by pouring the credit of the State freely into the housing market, has laid the groundwork for a disaster that will affect the majority of the people in this country; and that may eventually precipitate a severe economic downturn. The magnitude of the overexpansion of mortgage debt since 1976 has been so great that any attempt by an alarmed Government that suddenly realizes what it has done to forestall the impending collapse by propping up the prices of houses would be virtually certain to cause the rate of inflation to accelerate substantially.

These are the chief ingredients of the financial mess that the United States now finds itself in. The next questions to be asked are: what can, should, and is likely to be done about it?

Measures to slow our progress down the road to disaster

If we decide to continue down the road to inflationary disaster, the experiences of European social democracies suggest some useful measures that will at least slow our rate of descent. One measure that I recommend strongly in any case is the substitution of a value added tax, which is a national sales tax that is imposed at every stage of production and distribution, for the income tax.[2] It would be much better for our economy in several respects. Perhaps its most useful point of superiority in the situation that is developing in the United States is that it is much easier to levy a tax on at least part of the consumption of the people in the subterranean economy than it is to get at their incomes so that tax evasion would be much reduced and the steadily increasing unfairness of the present system would also be considerably mitigated. VAT also tends to discourage consumption but not saving and investment as the income tax does, so it would help to restore the international competitiveness of the American economy. It would also do that in a more direct way because VAT is rebated on exports and charged on imports. The United States has always maintained that this is unfair trade policy, a charge that the countries that use it have consistently rejected. If you can't beat 'em, join 'em. Should VAT become the principal method of personal taxation, as I recommend, it could be made a progressive tax by refunding all or part of it to people who are willing to swear that their income is not above a specified level. The clumsiness of what is generally called monetary policy and I prefer to call liquidity policy might also be mitigated by resorting

---

[2]In practice, VAT is just about as complicated as the income tax. To inflict both of them upon the American people would be a disaster that would condemn us to spend most of our working hours figuring taxes rather than doing something useful.

to what the British call the corset. This is a flat order to the banks (and it could be applied to other lenders as well) that their loans outstanding not rise by more than a specified percentage during a specified period of time.

It is also highly desirable that we have a complete Federal takeover of transfer payments and a nationwide equalization of the real living standard that they provide as soon as possible. The population of the country is already beginning to sort itself out so that in a few years' time productive people in the Northeast, for example, will live in Connecticut and New Hampshire; and unproductive people will live in and around the decaying cities of New York and Massachusetts where the transfer payments and social services are particularly liberal. This trend portends not only financial disasters but also an intensification of the social disaster that the post–social democracy migration in this country has already caused.

Finally, perhaps we should consider whether a change in the American constitutional framework is in order. Our Constitution was written in a simpler day, long before the advent of social democracy and totalitarian democracy. One of its chief goals was to make legislation a leisurely and thoughtful process because we used to think that laws should be wise rather than plentiful; and while the judiciary has been most ingenious at interpreting the Constitution to say many things that the people who wrote it would have considered to be insane, it has not been able to do very much about that. However, when the Government attempts to run the economy all kinds of things start to go wrong that require prompt legislative action. Strikes, for example, become political crises that require political solutions. And as inflation becomes endemic, policy has to wheel about repeatedly to confront first a rate of inflation that is becoming intolerable and then a rate of unemployment that is becoming politically intolerable. The legislature needs to be able to react quickly, and with the minimum of notice. European parliamentary governments can change the level of VAT or the size of the corset overnight, without giving the markets time to take evasive action. In Washington legislation is debated for months; and if our Congress tried to do those things everyone would anticipate the outcome—for example, by buying before VAT is raised and by borrowing before the corset is tightened—so that in the short run the effects would be the opposite of those intended.

On balance, I recommend that we do something decisive about halting the inflation instead of tinkering with the American constitutional order in the attempt to live with it.

The requisite conditions for price and financial stability

During the nineteenth century prices and the financial system were stable in the long run not only because financial instruments were convertible into money with intrinsic value so that fears about the future real value of financial claims were translated promptly into a deflationary drain of coins and bullion out of the financial system, but also because borrowing and lending were recognized to involve real risks for the people and institutions that engaged in them. Neither the economy nor the financial system was considered to be guaranteed, and both the people who borrowed for unproductive purposes and the lenders who financed irresponsible borrowers could easily go broke. Thus the stability of the financial system and of the general price level were supported by the prudent self-interest of borrowers and lenders alike in avoiding bankruptcy. Both credit risks and liquidity risks were known to be real, and the occasional short-run financial crises and panics that characterized the nineteenth century reinforced the determination to minimize both of them by borrowing and lending prudently.

Today we have accidentally short-circuited all of the stabilizing mechanisms that were built into the nineteenth century financial system by the political attempt to guarantee everybody against all risks; and until the inevitable adverse financial consequences began to develop we did not foresee that this attempt to overstabilize the financial system would be disastrous because the theoretical descriptions of the system failed to inform us that a reasonable degree of risk was essential to its overall stability. Money with intrinsic value is gone for the foreseeable future, but the prudent self-interest of borrowers and lenders in keeping the rate of debt formation moderate and noninflationary could easily be restored by a deliberate policy of reintroducing the requisite awareness that finance is a risky business. If that awareness is not restored by policy, it is very likely to be restored by a series of financial calamities in spite of policy.

How to get off the road to financial disaster

Both domestic and international considerations dictate a deliberate, cold turkey Central Bank policy of refusing to create all the liquidity that the market demands in order to break the momentum of inflationary expectations before they overwhelm what little stability our financial system still possesses. That is the essential first step. It is a hard and painful one, particularly since the Fed has almost but not quite taken it three times before so that the next time financial market participants will not cease to do inflationary things for a long while because they will expect the Fed to relent as soon as the going gets tough. The only reason for taking this step is that the alternatives are worse.

If the Fed does not make bank credit unavailable at the margin it is eventually likely to become unavailable in the domestic market anyway because the inflation will continue to undermine confidence in the external value of the dollar; and sooner or later borrowing dollars in order to sell them short will appear to be so much more profitable than borrowing for more constructive purposes that dollar hedgers will be willing and able to outbid other borrowers by offering a higher interest rate than they can afford to pay. If that is what happens, then credit will become very scarce and expensive in the United States; but the external value of the dollar is likely to continue to fall. On the other hand, if the creation of bank credit is limited so severely by deliberate policy that financial managers begin to worry about the liquidity of their institutions, and therefore refuse to make additional loans or refinance existing ones, the domestic consequences will be much the same; but people and businesses that have sold dollars short will have to buy them back in order to repay their loans. In that case the external value of the dollar will recover, and the threat of a major slide in the American standard of living will be averted.

The Fed wants to avoid making credit marginally unavailable if that is at all possible because it will be blamed for all the painful domestic consequences, which are virtually certain to include a collapse in the prices of houses and a severe reduction in consumer spending. But it really has no choice. The domestic and the international consequences of the excessive rate of debt formation that has been fueled by the ready availability of bank credit in the United States are both becoming disastrous. A policy of simply pushing up nominal interest rates in the United States to new records will not work, for two reasons. The first is that the level of nominal interest rates that would be required to reduce the demand for credit in the face of the ongoing rate of inflation would also produce a disastrous rate of disintermediation from the domestic financial system. And the second reason is that until confidence in the dollar is restored by a convincing stabilization there is no feasible level of interest rates that will stop the speculation against it.

Moreover, next time the Fed cannot afford to fail. Since 1965 it has pushed the financial system to the brink three times, and each time it backed off when real trouble began to develop. In 1966 it relented when the bond market broke, and the last two times it relented when the most overextended borrowers went broke—in 1970 the Penn Central Railroad and in 1975 some of the Real Estate Investment Trusts—in each case before the financial community as a whole was scared into lasting prudence with respect to borrowing and lending. The next time the Fed will have to squeeze until even some reasonably prudent people, businesses and financial institutions are badly hurt—and everyone is thoroughly frightened. If the Fed is not willing to do that, then it is altogether probable that the foreign exchange market and/or the domestic financial market will do it because confidence in financial claims denominated in U.S. dollars will have reached the vanishing point. An administered crunch is no fun, but it is greatly to be preferred to an uncontrolled panic.

Once a remorseless squeeze has broken the grip of inflationary expectations, the next step is to prevent them from getting a renewed grip after the squeeze has been relaxed by reversing or pruning back to a financially viable size the political policies and programs that originally spawned them.

We have already reviewed most of the basic principles upon which such a retrenchment should be based. The excessive use of the credit of the Federal Government, and of many State and local governments, to achieve politically desirable goals like housing, the attempts to overstabilize and overguarantee the economy, to provide an excessively high level of incomes that are unrelated to productive contributions by means of transfer payments, and to mandate investments that the private sector would not make voluntarily, have all caused such untoward economic and financial consequences that they now constitute major threats to the standard of living in the United States.

Unfortunately, some of the most mischievous programs are also among the most popular. The politically fostered excessive financing of housing has not only produced a dangerous inflationary bubble in house prices, but also a serious misallocation of resources that we can no longer afford. Houses are generally considered to be capital assets, but they are not productive capital goods whose acquisition helps to restore American productivity and competitiveness so that this country can stop borrowing and start earning its way in the world again. Housing units are really very long-lived consumer goods; and until the fundamental international competitiveness of our economy is restored we cannot afford to go on devoting half of the long-term debt that is created in this country to financing them.

The Social Security program has also been popular because it was very profitable for people who retired in the 1930's, 1940's and 1950's after relatively few years of paying Social Security taxes. Now the untoward consequences that inadequate funding inevitably produce are beginning to develop; and the rules simply have to be changed sooner or later, or the burden of taxes upon the productive sector will rise to a level at which they will constitute an insurmountable disincentive to work.[3]

The Government regularly defaults in real terms, but it must not default in nominal terms

A fundamental principle in this area is that it is bad enough for the Federal Government to renege on its promises to the people in real terms through inflationary financing; it absolutely must not renege on them in nominal or money terms as well—or at the very least, it must do so as little as possible. Even some of the politicians who understand the problem, and know that something has to be done about it, would much prefer to wait until the Social Security system is virtually at the point of crisis before grasping the nettle and changing the rules. That is tantamount to deliberately misleading the people about the benefits that they can expect to receive. It is far better to change the rules as soon as possible, and as long before the time that the new rules will take effect, as possible.

Reform will be politically difficult because each of these programs and policies has developed a constituency to whom they are very important, while the benefits that would

---

[3]I recommend to your attention the booklet *Social Security: Prospect for Change,* by A. Haeworth Robertson (until recently the Chief Actuary of the Social Security Administration), published by William M. Mercer, Inc., in 1978.

result from abandoning or pruning them would accrue to the country as a whole. The losses to the constituencies would in most cases be direct and visible; the gains, while much larger overall, would be diffuse and obscure. Politicians naturally prefer to provide modest favors that the voters will recognize rather than substantial benefits that the people may not realize are the results of ceasing to try to do politically popular, but in the end financially impossible, things.

Financial turmoil will continue, at least for a while

It does not seem likely that either the present Administration or the present Congress will be willing to reverse these powerful and long-running trends to anything like the extent that would be necessary to reinforce the coming crunch and thereby restore lasting financial stability. So we are most probably in for continuing financial turmoil until 1981 at the earliest. On the other hand, the American people's awareness of the problems and of the urgent need to do something fundamental to resolve them, before the national standard of living begins to slide seriously, appears to be rising rapidly; and this book is an attempt to give it another upward nudge. It is reasonable to hope that the 1980 presidential and congressional elections will mark a decisive turn off of the road to financial disaster that we started down in 1960.

NINE

What Can You Do about It? Recommendations for Personal Policy

I hope that this book has helped you to understand the fundamental causes of the inflationary disaster toward which we are heading, and why it will be as politically difficult as it is financially, economically and socially imperative that we reverse the national policies that are propelling us toward disaster. The last question with which we must deal is how productive and responsible people are to cope with a world that no longer appears to value their productive contributions, and in which saving and investing in order to be able to discharge their future responsibilities have become unrewarding. It is not an easy question to answer because one of the chief consequences of endemic inflation is steadily growing instability and uncertainty. Let us first examine the trends and developments that do appear to be reasonably foreseeable.

The outlook for the 1980's

We have reviewed the process by which fads in inflation hedges get pushed too far on too much borrowed money and then collapse, producing a localized financial disaster; and I

133

have given you my reasons for believing that the next collapse will be in house prices, and the next financial disaster in the personal sector. The recent rate of debt formation strongly suggests that the consequences will be severe enough to produce a substantial shrinkage of consumer spending, and therefore a fairly serious recession.

Just when the decline in house prices and the recession will occur is unpredictable because they will most probably be triggered by an unexpected shock that causes people to become more worried about the size of their debts than they are about the damage that inflation is doing to the real value of their incomes and savings. World political order is declining very rapidly now, and there are many wars and crises going on any one of which could precipitate a collapse of confidence; but exactly which one will turn out to be the last straw is anybody's guess.

Speaking in more general terms, the real standard of living in the United States is virtually certain to fall moderately in the short run because it will be impossible to go on much longer borrowing, from people who would prefer to reduce their loans to the United States, in order to import more petroleum than we can pay for out of external earnings. It has been perfectly obvious since the end of 1973 that something had to be done; and if that long period of time had been used wisely we would now be importing most of our petroleum from Canada and Mexico. Both countries have problems, but they are far more stable than the Middle East; and they need real goods and services that we could supply them in exchange for oil and gas. That would be a much sounder approach than is continuing mindlessly to give the OPEC countries enormous additional claims against the United States, the real value of which will remain doubtful for many years to come.

However, instead of reaching an accommodation with Canada and Mexico we frittered the time away; and by now the enormous accumulation of dollar-denominated claims against the United States poses the threat of a severe decline in our national standard of living caused by another collapse in the external value of the dollar. The main reason for hoping that that will not occur is that political stability is declining, and the level of violence is rising, much more rapidly in many other parts of the world than they are here; and are stimulating a sizable demand for dollars with which to buy real assets in this country. We will return to the implications of this trend for your own investments at the end of this chapter.

Social democracy works well for a generation or two at most

A third problem that we will have to face up to during the 1980's stems from the fact that social democracy only works well in its early stages when it can provide the resources for excessive consumption by running down the real productive capital that it inherited, and before it has eroded the habits of working, saving and investing that were worthwhile in the preceding era but that become progressively less rewarding as social democracy develops. In a social democracy the governmental sector creates excessive debt in order to finance transfer payments, and therefore consumption; and then the private sector goes into debt to finance both consumption and the acquisition of inflation hedges, which are seldom productive tools. Real productive capital is not accumulated at a satisfactory pace, and existing productive assets are not adequately maintained; with the consequence that sooner or later the productive side of the economy begins to fall apart. By now even those showplaces of social democracy, the Scandinavian countries, are finding it increasingly difficult to maintain economic productivity. Since there no longer exist adequate incentives for working hard it is necessary to find disincentives for not working; and in Sweden they are trying to figure out how to put a tax on leisure.

In the United States one area in which the long-standing

failure to maintain real capital has finally caused an extremely serious problem is public transportation. The Government has prevented the railroad industry from following economically sound policies or charging adequate rates for generations, and now many of the railroads are on the verge of breaking down. Many other forms of public transportation are also in sufficiently bad condition that they are becoming unreliable.

Think carefully about where you are going to live

The current high prices of houses, the vulnerability of a large part of our gasoline supply, and the growing unreliability of much of our public transportation all suggest that you ought to give careful consideration to the question of finding a safe, convenient and satisfactory place to live. It is clear that social democracy has made many areas in our older cities unfit places for any productive person to live, and during the 1980's those areas will grow and spread to the older and less desirable neighborhoods in the suburbs. Many elderly people who have retired on fixed incomes, and thus have lost the flexibility of a wide range of options, are trapped in those areas because until disaster developed they thought that rent control was a favor to them. They now live in terror, and you do not want to be trapped with them.

There are many suburban areas that so far have managed to remain orderly and safe by the expedient of maintaining large police forces that patrol diligently; but if the houses are aging and becoming expensive to maintain, the public transportation is becoming unreliable, and there are devastated or deteriorating areas nearby, it is likely to prove a temporary expedient. Since the people with sufficient income and assets to have options will move out early, the police force will become increasingly expensive for those who remain; and eventually the town will become a trap.

The inflation-hedging boom in real estate has pushed the

prices of houses in many areas that, in my judgment, are headed for disaster up to amazing levels. If you own one of them and are in a position to do without a house for a while, selling out and renting in a safer area may be one of the best steps, both financially and personally, that you ever took.

A good time to think about this is when you approach age fifty-five. The children have left the nest so you don't need so large a house; and the internal revenue code now permits you to realize a profit of up to $100,000 on the sale of your house, without having to pay a capital gains tax, if you are fifty-five or older. Remember that you can do this only once—you cannot carry forward any unused portion of the $100,000—so if you are buying a much more expensive house that you will eventually wish to sell, it may make sense to go ahead and pay the capital gains tax on the sale of your present house. However, in my opinion, after the current boom breaks it is likely to be quite a while before many people again have large capital gains on houses.

The apocalyptic school and the German experience

While we are on the subject of places to live, let me mention that there is an apocalyptic school that is gaining increasing attention today and that flatly predicts total financial and social disaster. Therefore it advocates not only defensive investments but a defensive life-style as well, and recommends buying a farm in the country, a rifle and a generous supply of canned foods. Anything you have left over should be converted into gold and buried in the cellar.

If you are personally convinced that we are headed for Armageddon, or if events after 1980 make it seem probable, then that would indeed be the best policy, as is evidenced by the facts that the only people who came through the series of disasters that Germany suffered between 1914 and 1948 in any kind of comfort at all were the farmers; and just about the only other assets beside farms that survived both the inflation and the following deflation were gold coins. Personally, the thing that impresses me most about the German experience is the wirtschaftswunder—the economic miracle, which in 1948 looked wildly improbable—that pursuing sound national policies after that year produced. My strongest recommendation is that you vote in 1980 for politicians who will introduce similar policies here—and expect similar results when they do. If a miracle was possible in the Germany of 1948 it is possible anywhere, and certainly it is in the United States. It is worth trying at least once more to get this country, which not too long ago was the most productive and progressive one in the world, back on the track before you give up and decide to try to sit out total disaster in the countryside.

However, if we fail to restore financial stability after 1980 and you decide to give up on urban civilization, there are a few differences between Germany in the 1920's and the United States in the 1980's that you should take into consideration in choosing your retreat. The urban Germans who faced starvation in the fall of 1923, participated in the political violence of the Weimar era, and faced about equal chances of starving or freezing in the bitter winter of 1947–1948 lived in apartments, and did not have automobiles. Railroad transportation was for all practical purposes free in 1923 because the fares had not been raised since before the war, but it was nowhere near as easy for the desperate urban mobs to penetrate into the agricultural hinterland as it would be for their contemporary American counterparts. Looting of farms certainly occurred in Germany at times, but it was far less prevalent than it would be in this country in similar circumstances.

Before the coming of the snowmobile isolated rural houses used to be left more or less alone, at least during the winter in the snowier parts of the country; but today that is no longer so. The urban Americans who would be hurt the most by serious social disorder are far more mobile than the Germans were, and they will remain so until the last gallon of gasoline is used up. There are very few areas remaining in the United States in which you could leave an unoccupied house stocked with food and weapons, let alone gold, and expect to find it unmolested when you needed it. Today a rural retreat would have to be guarded; and if chaos does develop it would have to be either extremely remote or easily defended to serve the purpose. A good farm, with its fields and outbuildings, is usually not easy to defend. A French farmhouse is typically built of stone and is virtually a fortress as it stands, but there is nothing so combustible as the typical American farmhouse and barn; and it is worth remembering that arson appears to be becoming the favorite sport in the older and more decrepit American cities.

You want to find a farm in a cove far back in the hills; and preferably above a bridge that can be defended and, if necessary, destroyed. There are many such places in the United States, but they are usually very poor farms that sensible people gave up trying to cultivate long ago; and today many of them are very expensive because ski lodges and summer places are popular inflation hedges. If chaos does not develop, paying top dollar for a hardscrabble farm in a remote area is unlikely to prove to be a good investment. On the other hand, most of us like country places; and if you want to have one anyway, or already own one, the additional cost of equipping it as a redoubt can be modest. Personally, having had a nodding acquaintance with subsistence farming in New England during the Depression, I will cast my lot in with civilization until the odds look a lot worse than they do today. Planning to sit out a national disaster in rural comfort strikes me as being more romantic than practical for most of us.

However, if the outcome of the 1980 election is not satisfactory, elderly people may not have much choice. It depresses me to drive past the recently developed retirement villages in the Southeast that are in effect guarded stockades. I would much prefer to retire to one of the few places in this country that are sufficiently remote that such measures are unnecessary, and are unlikely to become necessary. I will not name my own favorite village because it is very small and has little potential for expansion; but if your thoughts run along similar lines, before making a final decision you should consider the quality and size of the local constabulary organization. Most rural police forces are adequately staffed to handle their normal problems, but are not equipped to cope with civil insurrection or massive looting.

Try to avoid retirement as long as possible

Unless you are already at or close to retirement age, do not count upon receiving indefinitely the real income that the Social Security system presently appears to promise you. The lack of proper funding, in combination with the rapid aging of the population, will make that impossible to maintain within the next quarter century because the payroll tax that would be required would demolish the already dangerously weakened incentive to work. The current proposal to shift some of the burden to the Federal Government's general revenues would not alter that fundamental situation to any significant extent. If you are covered by a corporate pension plan it is most probable that it is funded far more adequately than the Social Security system, but it is not probable that it can keep you whole in real terms during a serious inflation.

It is disheartening to realize that the goal of retiring at age sixty-five is becoming impracticable for most Americans, but that is the case. Unless the fundamental causes of inflation are decisively rooted out after 1980, most of us will find it advisable to arrange our careers so that the period in which we will be exposed to outliving our resources is minimized. It would be best if you can arrange to have your level of activity taper off gradually, but don't part company with earned income until you absolutely have to.

Depending on the nature of your profession, continuing to work after sixty-five may be a good idea anyway. That deadline was established when Bismarck first introduced a measure of social democracy in Germany a century ago. At that time very few people could expect to live very long or be very active after sixty-five. It makes a lot less sense today when improved medical techniques, and the much better care that a great many middle-aged Americans are taking of themselves now that we are beginning to understand how to combat the degenerative diseases, are considerably increasing their life expectancy. You are likely to be in better shape physically and emotionally as well as financially if you stay on the job as long as possible.

Working and saving are not obsolete

I said earlier that one of the most fundamental causes of our steadily worsening financial difficulties is the fact that social democracy and inflation appear to have made working, saving and investing unrewarding things to do. If you have made a practice of working hard, saving and investing in financial claims, and have not splurged on things that you could not really afford, you most probably now feel rather cheated and more than a little foolish. I know, for I am one of you. However, now is most emphatically not the time to change your habits. At the very least, we are almost certainly headed for a major financial crisis in the not too distant future, in which liquid savings will prove invaluable. And if it turns out that we are also headed for financial and social disaster, productive, self-reliant and foresighted people who have accumulated some savings will be far better equipped to cope with it than will those who are relying upon political promises because their options will be much more numerous.

The chief characteristics of an inflationary era are instability and uncertainty

Once inflation has become endemic, it also becomes very difficult to give advice about specific types of financial assets that is of sufficient permanence to be worth recording in a book. I have come close to telling you flatly to sell houses because they are at or near the peak of their popularity as inflation hedges, and those that are located in areas that will be seen to be vulnerable once the euphoria wears off are particularly susceptible to a crash. However, it is not always feasible to consider a house simply as a financial asset. We can take stocks and bonds or leave them alone, but most of us have to have a place to live.

Financial investments

With respect to specifically financial investments, recommended policies have to take account of two possibilities. In 1980 we will either elect a President and a Congress who are determined to stop the inflation because they know that it will lead to a disaster, or we will not. In the first case, it is clear that now will turn out to have been the best opportunity to buy fixed-income securities since the Battle of Waterloo in 1815. In the second case, the next Administration will experience British rates of inflation, intensifying financial crises, and a general environment in which it appears that nothing works right any more and that it is becoming progressively more difficult to get anything accomplished.

In the early stages of the inflation, the remaining vestiges of money with intrinsic value offered some remarkable opportunities for profit without risk. I was particularly partial to silver dollars, which at the beginning of the 1960's still circulated as money; and handsome American gold coins were available from coin dealers at a very modest premium over the fixed monetary value of gold, which was virtually certain to be raised eventually. Finally, by about 1963 it became clear that the U.S. Treasury silver certificate dollar bills would become worth more as receipts for silver than as money.

Alas, the only such opportunity remaining is a trivial one. It does appear that the copper penny is likely to be worth more as copper than as money sooner or later, but you are going to have to hoard an awful lot of pennies to make your fortune out of that.

What about gold?

What are the prospects for a restoration of the linkage between the financial system and money with intrinsic value that will create a large profit for people who buy gold even at today's high prices? *If* it happens the profit could indeed be large because the monetary value of gold would have to be raised considerably in order for the world's gold supply to constitute a plausible backing behind the enormous amount of liquid liabilities outstanding in the world today. In the United States the Federal Reserve banks used to be required to hold a gold reserve equal to at least 25 percent of their bank note and deposit liabilities; and as we have seen, in Germany before World War I the Reichsbank was required to keep a gold reserve of 33⅓ percent of its liabilities. In Switzerland even today the gold reserve ratio is 40 percent!

But it is wholly unlikely that the linkage will be restored, except perhaps as part of a fundamental reform of the financial system after a catastrophic smash, in which case there will be many other ways to gain or lose purchasing power. At today's prices precious metals are risky, just like everything else. However, gold is one of the very few things in the world that is certain to retain a substantial purchasing power value under any foreseeable circumstances, and many conservative people will want to have some now that it is again legal for Americans to own enough gold to matter. If you are interested in gold, then as a broad generalization the time to buy it is when the financial markets are calm, it looks as though nothing much is going wrong, and the price of gold has slumped considerably since the last crisis. When the next crisis comes and the price of gold hits a new high it is generally a good idea to sell it and put the proceeds into something that has been depressed by the crisis. By now there are no riskless investments (except the mechanically impractical example of copper pennies) and no long-term investments left. Endemic inflation produces steadily increasing instability, and forces you to live by your wits.

There are no long-term investments anymore

If you are smart enough, or intuitive enough, to discern what the next fad in inflation hedges is going to be, it will prove profitable to get in on it early as long as you remember that today there is no such thing as a permanent investment so that you also get out in time. I have never been very good at guessing what the next popular inflation hedge will be; but deciding when the fad has been carried too far is fairly easy. It makes greater demands upon one's character than upon one's brains because you have to follow your own judgment and do just the reverse of what most people are doing.

When to get out

The first and most important thing to look for is overvaluation. In the appendix you will find a very clear and specific forecast of the bear market of 1969–1970. Unfortunately, I failed to make the key point sufficiently explicit. In the middle of 1968 common stocks were selling at very high price/earnings ratios and very low yields, at a time when the yields on good-quality bonds had already reached the highest level in more than a century. Common stocks were clearly overvalued by a substantial margin, and therefore should have been sold. All the other reasons cited in the forecast are merely corroborative icing on the cake.

The next thing to look for is how much is being borrowed to finance the purchase of the popular inflation hedges. I have already pointed out that in 1967 and 1968 businesses were borrowing billions to buy up other businesses without issuing more common stock so that earnings per share would be increased in the process; and that in 1977 and 1978 mortgage debt upon houses increased by about $100 billion a year. The other things to look for are qualitative and psychological factors that tend to confirm your judgment based upon the two fundamental factors of value and leverage. One is the faith that in the long run the prices of this particular class of assets can only go up. People have repeatedly believed that about common stocks, and today they believe it about houses. The second is speculative fever. In the 1969 forecast I said, "The stock market appears to have topped out in a typical speculative orgy during 1968"; and in 1978 the market for new houses in California demonstrated a similar quality of frenzy. If you have a reasonable amount of level-headed common sense, and the courage to act on your own convictions, identifying speculative peaks is not difficult. Indeed, a prudent person will usually sell out too early; but that is far less bad than not selling out in time.

And when to get in

The approach to acquiring financial assets that I find to be the most useful, and that I recommend to people who are willing to make their own investigations and decisions, is to wait until a financial smash has occurred, and then try to determine whether it also has gone too far. For example, at the beginning of the 1970's the Guardian Life Insurance Company owned very few securities of electric utility companies because they were generally considered to be of high quality, and did not provide the yield that we demand. However, after the quadrupling of petroleum prices at the end of 1973 a panic developed in utility securities; and it was reinforced the next spring when the Consolidated Edison Company eliminated its common stock dividend. We took a careful look at the situation and decided that, while the superficial analogy with the railroads was obvious, both the legal and the economic position of the electric utility industry was so strong that the bulk of its securities were perfectly sound, and represented excellent value. By now about 27 percent of the Company's assets are invested in them.

An example of thinking for oneself

Electric utility companies are permitted to operate as monopolies because it is too expensive to go stringing competitive networks of wires around town. Since competition does not restrain the rates that they can charge, the rates are set by regulation. The panic was caused by fear that populist regulators would not permit the utility companies to recover the increased costs that inflation in general and the soaring cost of energy in particular were imposing upon them; and to a certain extent the fear was justified. However, in return for a limit on their profits the utilities are legally entitled to a reasonable return on the investment that they have devoted to the public service; and if necessary they can appeal to the courts to overrule the regulators. Moreover, as a practical matter demand for electricity is still growing, admittedly not as fast as we expected before 1973, so the utilities must continually attract new capital which they will not get if the return on the existing capital is unreasonably low. The utility industry was developed and financed after the Interstate Commerce Commission had begun the long slow process of destroying the railroad industry, and utility bond indentures are tightly written to prohibit the borrowing of more capital if the regulators attempt to do the same thing to it. Financiers may not be very bright, but we are capable of learning by experience.

Finally, electricity still costs far less than it is worth to the consumer. We all complain about our bills because they have gone up so much in recent years, but nobody yet drinks warm beer or skips his favorite television show in order to save on electricity. I believe that electric utility securities were, and still are, very attractive; and are particularly suitable both to the needs of a life insurance company and to individuals who require assured income. Until market conditions change I expect that the portion of our assets that is invested in them will continue to rise. The chance of a killing in the market appears to be small, but you never know. Lightning sometime strikes in strange places.

The crisis in the municipal bond market

For example, in the mid-1970's a localized financial crisis developed in the municipal bond market, largely because of the financial difficulties of New York City and State and the Commonwealth of Massachusetts all of which had done many social democratic things, including excessive borrowings to finance subsidized housing. Normally it does not make much sense for a life insurance company to buy municipal bonds because the very complex law under which we are taxed has the mathematical effect of imposing a tax on municipal bond interest. But the crisis forced both New York and Massachusetts to pay very high interest rates on several bond issues, some of which we believe to be adequately secured; and also depressed the market prices of other municipal bonds that were clearly sound.

Normally one does not buy municipal bonds in order to make a killing. But by early 1978 the closing of other income tax loopholes (in the eyes of the Internal Revenue Service, any income that a taxpayer gets to keep is evidence of a loophole) improved the relative attractiveness of municipal bonds, and several large mutual funds were formed to invest in them. This increased demand permitted us to sell for almost $56 million bonds that we had paid about $49 million for, resulting in a profit of nearly $7 million after a holding period that averaged about a year and a quarter, during which we had also received an excellent income upon our funds. In the process of taking losses in order to avoid paying taxes upon this large capital gain we were able to get rid of just about every investment that we had any doubts about, and thus to get our portfolio into excellent shape to withstand whatever vicissitudes lie ahead.

It is essential to think for yourself

The financial markets will remain unstable at least as long as the inflation lasts, and opportunities like these will occur repeatedly. But, in order to take advantage of them you must make your own analyses and draw your own conclusions. During the crisis in utility finance, which produced some of the best bargains in fixed-income securities in the history of this country, there was a standing joke in Wall Street about Utilities Anonymous—if you got the urge to buy a utility security you could call them up and somebody would talk you out of it. It is precisely this kind of professional group-think that dooms the majority of investment managers to mediocre results. If you are not personally capable of doing investment analysis and making investment decisions, these remarks will indicate the qualities that you should look for in an investment advisor. I also strongly recommend that you read Benjamin Graham's book *The Intelligent Investor*.[1] It is a little dated by now, but the attitude and approach that it recommends are absolutely sound.

Quality is also essential

I hope it is clear by now that you absolutely must insist on high quality in all your financial investments. Two decades of persistent overborrowing and overspending have left the financial system as a whole, and in virtually all of its parts, dangerously weakened. There was a considerable restoration of financial strength in the corporate sector after the debacle of 1970, but by now it has been dissipated again. There will eventually be a large number of personal and corporate bankruptcies, and probably some municipal bankruptcies as well. You want to look for something that the market considers to be risky, like the electric utility industry, but that you don't. This is not the time to be accepting real risks in exchange for a moderate increase in income.

Whenever U.S. Government bonds are yielding within 85 percent or more of the return on good-grade corporate bonds, the layman is probably well advised to confine his long-term fixed-income investments to them. The State is in principle the best credit in the country because it has the power to tax away all the wealth of the rest of us.

Stocks are better values than houses

While I would wait for the next crisis before taking a full position in common stocks, or anything else for that matter, I am inclined to take a very constructive view of the stocks of

---

[1]Fourth edition, Harper & Row, Publishers, Incorporated, New York, 1973.

large and *financially sound* American industrial and commercial enterprises. I especially like growth stocks, and that is a new departure for me. Back in the days when the recognized growth stocks sold at price/earnings ratios three or four times as high as those of more mundane businesses, I was very skeptical that one could be sure enough of the superiority of growth companies' prospects to justify paying that kind of a premium. Today, however, the premium that the market is willing to pay for the stocks of companies that are obviously outstandingly well run, and that operate in what have been growth markets that appear likely to remain so, strikes me as being ridiculously small.

In 1978 the external value of the dollar fell a great deal more than its internal value so that the United States today is a bargain hunter's paradise, particularly for people with strong currencies. The rest of the world also has a lot of highly liquid dollar-denominated claims against the United States whose real value is being constantly eroded by the American inflation. It makes a lot of sense to use them to buy the common stocks of sound American businesses that are currently very modestly priced even in terms of dollars. Foreign businessmen have already seen the point, and they are buying up whole businesses here at a record clip because the price is so reasonable.

When you are trying to buy a few shares rather than the whole business, you tend to take a different approach. If the market is going down there is a great temptation to wait for the bottom before you buy. This can turn out to be a mistake if the market gets away from you, and personally I put more emphasis on the reasonableness of the current price than on the trend of the market; but because of this psychological phenomenon I do not expect to see enormous foreign portfolio investment in American common stocks until the external value of the dollar has been convincingly stabilized. Nevertheless, it seems to me that as a class the stocks of financially sound American companies are the most attractive financial assets in the world today. Considered purely as financial assets, I would much rather own stocks than houses.

The Outlook for the Economy and the Securities Markets in 1969

A year of crises

I am managing the funds under my supervision in accordance with a rather dramatic view of the prospects for the securities markets and the general economy in 1969—a view to which I am quite firmly committed. I believe that during the next several months there will be an eyeball-to-eyeball confrontation between the business and financial community's confident belief in continued accelerating inflation and the Administration and the Federal Reserve Board's firm determination to slow it down virtually to the vanishing point. This in itself is not an extreme or unusual position; but I also believe that, after a full generation in which bets on inflation have always paid off, the inflationary psychology cannot be broken without some extremely severe economic and financial repercussions. We have already seen the entire spectrum of interest rates pushed up to a level that has no precedent since the greenback inflation during the Civil War when the survival not only of the monetary system but of the Union itself was in question; and the short run outlook is clearly for even higher rates across the board.

The stock market appears to have topped out in a typical speculative orgy during 1968. I believe that the trend turned definitely down in December; and that the most likely prospect is for a major bear market bearing some reasonable proportion to the long bull market that we have enjoyed since 1947. As the financial pressures intensify the explosive uptrend of spending by all levels of government will slow down abruptly, and the inflation-hedging expansion of business investment in fixed assets and inventories will go into reverse. Finally, I expect that the much battered and frequently mended international payments mechanism will collapse altogether within the next twelve to—possibly—eighteen months.

Another way of saying this is that in recent years we have invested a great deal of energy and ingenuity in sweeping a number of serious and growing problems under the rug, with the result that they will all reach crisis proportions more or less simultaneously as money and confidence run out. My view is not unrelievedly gloomy however. I anticipate that *after* all these crises have erupted, bold and imaginative, probably highly inflationary, steps will be taken to deal with them. However, I do *not* believe that investment policy should attempt to look beyond the period of crisis to the eventual inflationary recovery. I think it will prove far wiser and more profitable to remain defensive and liquid in the short run, and be in a position to pick up the clear bargains when the majority that believed it could not happen again is paralyzed with shock and fear.

This is, as I commented at the outset, a very dramatic thesis. It is good theater even if it turns out to be bad economics. In defending it I will briefly review the monetary developments of the last quarter century in order to stress both the secular nature of the trends that appear to be reaching a climax this year and the degree to which they have pervaded and shaped our economy and society. The major emphasis will be on the economic and financial aspects, but I hope that an occasional glance at the political and social implications will be forgiven. And if it appears that I am harping on basic and obvious fundamentals it is because our national policies and attitudes have remained too long under the spell of sophisticated but erroneous doctrines from which they are just beginning to emerge.

A fundamental assumption: human nature doesn't change very much

In most reviews of this sort the writer's basic philosophical beliefs about the subject at hand usually emerge in the last paragraph or chapter as the clear lessons to be learned from the course of events that have been analyzed. I will attempt to lay bare my profoundest thoughts about monetary economics at the outset, and then discuss how recent economic history appears from that point of view.

It has always seemed to me that the combination of human nature and a credit economy is dynamite. When things are going well, a system that allows people who have a productive use for economic wealth to borrow readily from those who have an excess facilitates a rate of economic growth that was inconceivable as long as wealth consisted mainly of tangible material goods that could not be transferred easily or efficiently. But such a system is also inherently unstable. Once human beings have discovered that they can create economic claims out of thin air by the extension of credit, and that doing so usually results in the miraculous production of the tangible goods and services that validate the claims, it then becomes more or less inevitable that they will push the process too far. An accelerated rate of credit formation is a wonderful stimulus to productive activity; but once the quantity of claims that have been created gets seriously out of balance with the tangible wealth on which it is supposed to rest, lenders grow suspicious and overextended borrowers get scared. Then loans are called, borrowers default and the contraction of credit also retards the production of real, tangible wealth. After each such crisis new restraints and palliatives are invented—for example, bank reserve requirements to slow down the pace of credit formation and deposit insurance to ameliorate its contraction. But until human beings become cold-bloodedly rational, immune both to excessive optimism and unreasoning fear, I do not see how the credit cycle can be abolished entirely without also abolishing economic growth.

RECENT MONETARY HISTORY—A THUMBNAIL SKETCH

The suppressed inflation of the war years and its natural consequences

Let us start our review at the bottom of the cycle. The United States suffered a massive contraction of credit in the early 1930's, and business activity did not fully revive until the extreme demands of World war II came along. During the war the Government made liberal use of financial incentives to redirect civilian activities into war production; but at the same time it severely rationed the flow of goods and services into the civilian sector. With incomes up and the opportunities for spending down, most people perforce saved money. The Government also held down the interest cost of financing the war to what it considered a reasonable level by more or less forcing the banks to take huge amounts of Government bonds at 2½ percent.

Even before the war the civilian economy had been starved of goods and services for a decade by the Depression so that there was a considerable backlog of material needs to be satisfied in the postwar period. When you add to these conditions the fact that well into the postwar era the Central Bank remained obligated to turn the Federal debt back into relendable money by purchasing those 2½ percent Government bonds at par, it was clear that the stage was set for a major inflationary boom. (Oddly, the majority view at the time was that after the "extraordinary" demands of the war had subsided the country would sink back into the Depression. A more ludicrous misreading of the fundamentals can hardly be imagined. But it is typical of the major secular turns in the economic tide that the view of the sound majority is completely wrong.)

At the end of the war the burden of debts was extremely low

One of the conditions that facilitated the rapid postwar reconversion and the economic progress of the years 1946–1957 was that at the beginning of the period the level of (non-Federal) debts was very low in relation to incomes and to liquid assets. The commercial banking system was almost unbelievably liquid. Loans totalled only about 19 percent of deposits, and the banks' largest asset was Government bonds which could readily be turned back to cash with little or no loss. When the financing requirements of reconversion made it possible to buy good corporate bonds at 3¼ percent and to make sound mortgage loans at 4 percent, the banks dumped their Governments back on the Fed and jumped at the opportunity because it was clear that—in an economically mature, capital-rich but demand-poor country like the United States—such attractive rates were clearly a consequence of the unusual demands of the reconversion period, and wouldn't last very long.

1958–1961: the years of economic "normalcy"

The inflationary expansion of 1946–1957 was therefore a more or less natural and expectable consequence of the backlog of needs and demands piled up during a decade and a half of depression and war, combined with the hyperliquidity that resulted from the high level of savings and the low-interest-cost Federal financing of the war years. In my judgment, this process (complicated and prolonged by the Korean war episode) had pretty well worked itself out by 1957. The backlog of unsatisfied needs had largely been made good; the economy had grown into a reasonable balance with the war-swollen money supply; and municipal, corporate and individual debts had risen sharply into what struck me as a normal, reasonable and sustainable relationship with the level of incomes.

It seems to me that if any period since the Harding era can be described by his word for the golden age—"normalcy"— it was the years 1958–1961. I think that we saw then what the United States economy would look like if it were not stimulated by war or deliberate Federal medication, or affected by the aftermath of cataclysmic events. Politically and socially as well as economically, the period just felt like the classical economist's word for nirvana—"equilibrium." Granted that this is a subjective and qualitative view, what sort of evidence can be offered for it?

In comparison with the postwar years 1946–1957, the rates of real economic growth and of inflation both eased off. Unemployment rose during the recession of 1958 and then stabilized at nearly 6 percent of the workforce. Even so the standard of living, for the vast majority of Americans, was at an unprecedented peak. Indeed, when the nonquantitative factors of personal security, order and the general wholesomeness of the environment are taken into consideration, it is hard to argue that the general standard of living has made any real progress since then.

The only worrisome sign of potential instability in those years was the emergence of a substantial international payments deficit as Continental Europe and Japan completed their postwar reconstruction and again became formidable competitors in world markets. The payments deficit was certainly not alarming in view of the enormous liquid resources that the United States possessed at the time, but it did suggest that renewed domestic inflation might eventually cause real trouble.

The Kennedy Era and the New Economics

This combination, of a stable prosperity that the United States had not experienced in at least a generation with a relatively low rate of growth and relatively high unemployment, touched off a Great Debate among economists and politicians about whether stability was good enough. The issue was resolved in the negative in the Fall of 1960 when John F. Kennedy was elected President on a platform of Getting the Country Moving Again. This platform eventually blossomed out in full glory as the "New Economics."

When the doctrines of the New Economics are stripped of some statistical innovations such as the full employment surplus, it becomes clear that there is nothing new about them at all. Students of political economics have long known that a persistent Government deficit, combined with an easy money policy that encourages a rapid rate of debt formation, will powerfully stimulate economic activity—for a while anyway. The only serious question that conservative economists raised is whether we had now become so wise that the massive stimulation being applied to the economy could be gradually reduced as we approached full employment so that we would enjoy a prolonged boom rather than the temporary surge and eventual deflationary collapse that such policies had usually produced in the past.

My own view is that the New Economics was just the latest and most sophisticated version of the perennial illusion. I believe that by the mid-1960's there was definite statistical evidence that debt ratios were rising at an unsustainable rate and that we were clearly headed for trouble. But alas, we will never know. There is no controlled experiment in Economics—some extraneous event always comes along to upset the laboratory apparatus.

1965–1968: overstimulation and inflation

In this case, it was the sudden escalation of our military commitment in Vietnam in the summer of 1965. Until then the New Economics looked like an outstanding success. Real economic growth accelerated and unemployment fell, at the cost of a moderate rebirth of inflation and a continued balance of payments deficit that was successfully financed through a series of ingenious ad hoc arrangements. But from

1965 on the Johnson Administration's persistent failure to face up realistically to the economic impact of Vietnam resulted in a far greater degree of fiscal stimulation than even the most enthusiastic New Economist would have prescribed. The Governors of the Federal Reserve Board cried "wolf" at regular intervals but—except for an alarming episode in 1966—they continued to finance a mammoth expansion of the credit structure. The clear and obvious consequence has been that for the better part of three years now the American economy has been pushed beyond effective full employment and into true, classical inflation.

The startling events of 1968

By the first quarter of last year it looked as if the game was about over. Our commitment in Vietnam appeared to be a bottomless pit from which the Johnson Administration could not or would not extricate itself in spite of the surging tide of dissent that seemed to be escalating toward open rebellion. With inflation rampant and the United States budget apparently out of control, a major run out of sterling and the dollar into gold and the Continental currencies had developed and threatened to overwhelm the battered remains of the Bretton Woods monetary system. The American stock exchanges broke sharply in the first quarter, and it's hard to think of a more justified market slump than that one appeared to be.

The two bombshells exploding almost simultaneously that transformed market sentiment were Mr. Johnson's announcement that he would not run for reelection but would try to negotiate a settlement in Vietnam; and the civil insurrection in France, which far surpassed anything that has yet happened here. The first of these triggered an explosive peace rally in the American stock markets that tapered off during the third quarter and fizzled out altogether at the end of November. The second turned out to be the first in a series of events that shook investors' confidence in foreign economies and securities markets, thus reemphasizing the fundamental political and economic attractiveness of the

United States as a refuge for nervous money. The combination of these two events gave the international monetary system another year's lease on life; but as this is being written it is visibly sliding into a renewed crisis.

THE SCENE AT THE BEGINNING OF THE NIXON ERA: THE PROSPECTS FOR PEACE AND INFLATION

Two major psychological forces dominated the securities markets in the last three quarters of 1968. The first was the hope for an early settlement in Vietnam that would relieve the financial pressures generated by the Johnson Administration's disastrous budget calculations and would permit us to concentrate our attention on repairing the sadly raveled fabric of domestic life in the United States. The second was the fear of—or hope for—continued accelerating inflation. I believe that the markets' expectations are doomed to disappointment on both counts.

Vietnam and official hypocrisy

The contrast between what our political leaders are telling us and the conclusions suggested by simple observation and common sense can seldom have been more striking—even under totalitarian regimes—than it is with respect to Vietnam. Officialdom reports that the Communist forces have been so badly hurt by our military efforts that they are now ready to negotiate a mutually acceptable settlement. Indeed, the Johnson Administration claimed that it has already negotiated a significant de-escalation of the fighting—we have quit bombing North Vietnam in exchange for a freeze on the rate of infiltration into the South and a reduction in overt attacks on military and civilian targets.

The evidence supporting these points looks extremely feeble to me; and the contradictory evidence seems overwhelming. There is some reason to believe that the number and quality of Communist troops in the South have declined over the last twelve months; but on the other hand their weapons have obviously been getting steadily more sophisticated, more effective and more plentiful. There is not one iota of hard evidence that either the Government of North Vietnam or the Viet Cong is willing to settle for anything less than a complete American withdrawal under conditions that will enable them to take over the South in due course.

The position of the United States Government regarding the bombing halt is simply incredible. The North Vietnamese have steadily insisted that it was a unilateral and unconditional concession by the United States—that there never was any reciprocal "understanding." Since the significance of an entente that is not merely repudiated by one of the parties but whose very existence is flatly denied is doubtful in the extreme, it seems clear that Washington has been insisting on its validity mainly for reasons of domestic politics. Mr. Nixon is shortly going to have to decide what to do about the fact that North Vietnam's actions are entirely consistent with their version of the bombing halt. How much simpler his decision would be if, instead of endorsing the previous Administration's position, he had stated frankly that the "understanding" was a fabrication that did not bind him any more than it did Hanoi!

THE WAR ON INFLATION

We have had varying degrees of inflation for most of the last thirty-five years. Our political leaders and monetary authorities have steadily deplored it, and occasionally they have tried to alleviate some of its symptoms through wartime controls and peacetime "guidelines"—but only once in recent years have they attempted to do something decisive about its causes. This was during the famous "credit crunch" of 1966. Its impact on the securities markets scared the Federal Reserve Board so badly that as soon as a little steam started to leak out of the economy toward the end of the year, they promptly rushed to the other extreme and provided the banking reserves that supported a massive expansion of the money supply. The contrast between the Board members' verbal warnings about the dangers of inflation and their actual deeds in fuelling a true monetary inflation during 1967 and a good part of 1968—when the economy was virtually at full employment and the Federal Budget appeared to be completely out of control—was striking indeed; and its consequences are still plaguing us. It was the last straw that convinced even previously skeptical business and financial people that inflation is permanent and irreversible. Now a new Administration tells us that it is going to disinflate but not deflate; and ever since the votes were counted in November the Fed has been turning the screws down rather firmly. But, after a quarter century during which much has been said about inflation and little has been done, why on earth should we believe that they mean business this time?

Prolonged inflation is harmful in three distinguishable ways; and I think it is becoming quite clear that the American society and economy are beginning to be seriously damaged on all three counts. *If* the current attempt to stem inflation fails, then the momentum of inflationary expectations is indeed likely to become so powerful that it will be irreversible until it precipitates a crash that transforms our society as profoundly as Germany was by the consequences of their runaway inflation in the 1920's. I sense that both the monetary authorities and the important members of the Nixon Administration's economic team share this feeling that we are approaching a major watershed. They are all more or less conservative in their basic values; and I believe that they have reached the conclusion, not necessarily entirely conscious or clearly defined in their own minds, that we have come to the last opportunity to forestall a radical and catastrophic transfiguration of our culture.

The three respects in which inflation will eventually cause serious damage to a society are: an erosion of national independence and power, a growing risk of a deflationary collapse, and a decay of moral discipline and political order.

The following three sections[1] will analyze each of these in general terms, and then assess their current status in the United States. Then I will state my reasons for believing that the announced policy of disinflation without deflation is unlikely to work smoothly or painlessly. Finally, peering earnestly into my crystal ball I will try to discern some of the probable consequences of this major change in economic policy.

Relative rates of inflation, international monetary money flows and national power

Any nation that maintains both a fixed value for its money in relation to foreign currencies, and persistently indulges in a more rapid rate of inflation than its neighbors do, will eventually run into trouble of one sort or another. The fact that the prices of domestically manufactured goods are rising more rapidly than those of similar imported goods causes the inhabitants to spend more on imports and less on the local products, while the country's export markets shrink correspondingly. Domestic production, employment and incomes will be depressed. If the country has relatively free and competitive markets, and a government that refrains from taking defensive steps or offsetting the decline with stimulative monetary and fiscal policies, classical economic theory tells us that the resulting deflation will reduce the domestic price structure and restore equilibrium. Unfortunately, the theory has seldom worked very well in practice; and modern governments are unlikely to tolerate a dose of depression and deflation as long as there are any other alternatives left. Once embarked on the inflationary course, they are more likely to counteract any economic slowdown with a further dose of inflation.

Continued inflation after the balance of trade has begun to

---

[1] The third section is omitted in the interest of brevity. The points it made are by now obvious.

deteriorate necessitates defending the domestic economy by taxing imports and subsidizing exports; limiting the physical quantity of imports by quotas or prohibiting them altogether; or raising the domestic price of imports and lowering the external price of exports by exchange devaluation.

A current prescription—flexible exchange rates

If exchange rates are *not* fixed by Government action but are left free to be set by market forces, an unfavorable trend in the balance of payments will theoretically be counteracted by a fall of the value of the country's money in relation to foreign currencies. This would have the merit of making the adjustment process gradual and automatic; and in theory it would eliminate crises caused by speculative flights out of one currency into another. Therefore, some monetary economists are suggesting that we adopt such a policy so that we can continue to inflate at home without painful international consequences. The current talk about "wider gold points" and "crawling pegs" is a sophisticated attempt to combine this automatic adjustment mechanism with the greater ease of making commercial calculations and financing international trade that fixed exchange rates provide. Both ideas are ingenious, but both are capable of being sabotaged by unwise financial policies. For example, Canada had a floating exchange rate between the end of the War and 1962; and therefore according to the current theory she should never have run into balance of payments difficulties. But a catastrophic central banking policy during the late 1950's kept interest rates artificially high to combat inflation and thereby attracted a massive inflow of foreign capital that pushed the Canadian dollar to an overvalued level, caused a huge payments deficit, and eventually culminated in a run on the Canadian dollar and devaluation. (The story has a happy ending—pegging the dollar at a reasonable level and appointing a competent head of the Bank of Canada, just as world markets for their exports were starting to grow again, resulted in a powerful and sustained expansion of the Canadian economy.)

Whether exchange rates are fixed or free, once the citizenry become aware that the value of their money is likely to fall in relation to foreign currencies (either through depreciation or devaluation—it makes no great difference) they will try to get their surplus capital out of the country and into a sounder currency. Defending against this perfectly logical and natural process necessitates capital controls; and a policy of borrowing back the money that has already escaped, if the country's credit standing makes that possible.

The United States is a special case

The United States is in a unique position in this respect. Our price inflation since the late 1940's has been considerably less, when expressed in terms of percentage rates, than that in many other countries. Nevertheless our balance of trade has shrunk from a massive surplus to approximate balance, while capital has been flowing out of the country in sizable amounts. The reasons for this paradox are somewhat complex; but the matter is so important that it demands a brief analysis.

In the first place, our large trade surplus during the years of the dollar gap was caused not so much by relative prices as by simple availability. The United States emerged from World War II with the *only* large and productive industrial economy in the world that had not been devastated; and our generous foreign aid policies provided the continent of Europe and Japan with the money to buy from us what they needed to get going again. In spite of the theory of a permanent dollar shortage that was popular in the early 1950's, the closing of the dollar gap was a natural consequence of successful economic reconstruction—which was largely financed by the United States.

In the second place, there is a fallacy in the comparison of relative rates of price inflation when you start from substantially different base levels. I have studied the price trends in the steel and chemical industries here and abroad during the post-war period. In both cases prices have gone up a good deal less, percentage-wise, here than overseas; but the foreign levels were so much lower to begin with that the differential—in absolute dollars and cents terms—has actually widened. I suspect that this is also true for a great many other industrial products. Because we started out with a considerable price handicap we would have had to have a much lower rate of inflation than obtained in Japan and on the Continent if we were to hold on to our trade surplus after their postwar economic reconstruction was completed.

Money is power

Finally, a persistent trade surplus is just as unstable as a deficit *unless* the excess capital is put to good use abroad. The only sound reason for the United States to wish to retain a large surplus is that ever since the late 1940's it has been our policy to play a major role in shaping the course of world events—and that takes money. Neither the United States nor any other country can in the long run spend substantially more money abroad than it earns there. Our foreign aid, external capital investments and troop garrisons abroad all have to be financed either by surplus earnings or by borrowing. Our ability to pay for all the things that we think it is desirable to do abroad out of surplus foreign earnings has long since been eroded by inflation. So in recent years we have progressively restricted private and corporate foreign investment, and covered a steadily larger portion of the cost of the Government's external undertakings by borrowing abroad.

We can keep this up only as long as our national credit remains good—as long as foreign central banks are willing to lend their net accumulations of dollar back to us and foreign individuals want to invest their surplus dollars on the New York Stock Exchange. Just a year ago it looked as if our credit was running out; but then—thanks to Danny the Red and the French students and workers—France's credit rating suddenly fell even lower than ours; and we have been able to finance for one more year. But the end of the road is clearly in sight. Every year our ability to influence events beyond our borders is steadily more dependent on borrowing in an international market that is becoming progressively more strained and overextended. Eventually we will have to decide either to go out of the world power business—bring our troops home, cut back foreign aid and close up the World Bank—or to compete more effectively in world markets. The most probable answer will be a little of both—but we must reach some decision very soon; before foreigners decide that the United States is hopelessly profligate, present their claims for redemption in goods and services, foreign currency or gold; and thereby precipitate a major international monetary crisis.

THE DOMESTIC CONSEQUENCES OF INFLATION

So much for the international implications of inflation in the United States. Now let's see what it is doing at home.

The growing risk of a deflationary shrinkage of credit: the mechanics of inflation

The inflationary process can be defined very simply. It is the expansion of money purchasing power at a faster rate than that at which the real output of goods and services is growing. Unfortunately, the processes by which this disparity have been produced in the United States are somewhat complex. A quick excursion into basic monetary theory should throw some light on them and provide us with a framework within which to estimate how far we have come from the impregnable monetary conditions of the 1940's and early 1950's toward a situation in which a deflationary contraction of credit is not only possible but rather probable.

Any Government that is powerful enough to force its own people to use its notes as money can create an inflationary excess of purchasing power over real output simply by printing up a new batch of bills and spending them in addition to the money it has taken away from the private economy by taxation. A more sophisticated way of accomplishing the same result is to finance a budget deficit by selling its debt obligations to the banks. This works in the following manner: when I deposit a dollar in the bank, it is credited to my account and I can withdraw it and spend it any time I want to. If the Government then gives the bank its note and borrows my dollar, the bank credits the dollar to the Government's account too (balancing its books by carrying the Government's note as an asset) and—hey, presto!—two dollars of purchasing power exist where there was only one before. This increase is not necessarily cancelled when one of us spends his dollar, since it usually turns up immediately in somebody else's bank account.

Actually, it doesn't take the power of the Government to turn this trick. *Any* net expansion of municipal, corporate and/or individual debts that creates new liquid assets in anybody's hands, without correspondingly reducing the amount that somebody else can spend, increases purchasing power. In the United States the largest part of new liquid claims are created by the commercial banks' granting loans and crediting them to the borrowers' checking accounts. The only really important difference between an expansion of purchasing power that results from an increase in the Government's debt and one that results from a rise in the net indebtedness of the private sector is that the former is a unified process that can be accurately controlled while the latter results from a myriad of individual decisions that the Authorities can powerfully influence but not precisely control.

Since the end of the War commercial bank credit has risen 900 percent—from $26 billion in 1945 to $258 billion at the end of 1968—just three times as fast as current-dollar Gross

National Product or any other broad measure of incomes has grown. And virtually all other forms of non-Federal debt have grown much faster.

As long as the economy has a substantial reserve of unemployed people and other productive resources, the major part of any increase in purchasing power is used to hire the unutilized resources, and thus to expand real output. But as the economy approaches full employment it gets progressively more difficult to increase output quickly, and a steadily larger portion of the rising purchasing power just goes into bidding up prices. For example, in 1965 and 1966 real Gross National Product went up more than 6 percent per annum while prices rose about 2 percent a year. But in 1967 and 1968 as we approached closer to and finally reached effectively full employment the rate of increase in real Gross National Product dropped below 5 percent while the overall price level rose more than 3 percent on average. As far as we can tell, it is still climbing at an accelerating rate.

The factors limiting the growth of purchasing power

Conventional monetary theory describes two limitations upon the process of creating purchasing power through the expansion of bank credit. The first is the bankers' own prudent desire to maintain a sufficient stock of cash and assets of unquestionable liquidity to meet any reasonably expectable net withdrawals of deposit balances. The second is the Authorities' ability to manipulate the cash reserves that the banks are required to keep on deposit with the Central Bank. In our system, the Federal Reserve Board influences the rate of credit formation by raising or lowering the required reserve ratio, and by offering to buy or sell Treasury bills and (occasionally) other financial assets at prices that induce the banks to increase or decrease their holdings of cash reserves. If these techniques are wisely applied and succeed in keeping the rate of debt formation, and consequently the increase in purchasing power, in step with the rate at which real out-

put can expand, the result is likely to be sound, noninflationary growth and prosperity. But when purchasing power rises
more rapidly than real output, prices will go up. If the imbal-
ance appears to be a more or less permanent consequence of
imprudent financial policies, people will tend increasingly to
anticipate the upward spiral of prices and go ever more heavily into debt in order to buy at today's prices and pay up
with tomorrow's money.

The banking system has become dangerously illiquid

These two theoretical limitations upon the rate of debt formation have pretty well disappeared in recent years. As far
as the bankers' prudent self-interest is concerned, bankers
are no more immune than the next man to the inflationary
psychology and to the pervasive belief that Governmental
policies have taken the risks out of the economy. The traditional prudent maxim was—not more than 50 percent of
deposits in remunerative but doubtfully liquid loans; the
rest in vault cash, marketable treasury securities, short-dated
municipal bonds and prime-quality, marketable trade paper.
Today—if there is any limit at all—it must be loans not over
100 percent of deposits. (I can hardly conceive of the Authorities letting a commercial bank lend out its capital—but then
a few years back I would not have imagined that they would
permit loan/deposit ratios to reach the current level either.)
At year end the ratio for all commercial banks, adjusted to
eliminate interbank loans and deposits, was 63.6 percent.
And this is against a steadily more volatile structure of
resources. The Fed's refusal to raise Regulation Q and permit
the banks to pay a competitive rate on large Certificates of
Deposit has caused them to shrink in the last couple of
months. They have been replaced to some extent by Eurodollar advances from the banks' overseas branches, which
are about the most unstable liabilities imaginable. (However, the Eurodollar liabilities appear on the Balance Sheet as
Other Liabilities not as Deposits—so to that extent the loan/

deposit ratio isn't quite as high as it appears.) In January the C.D. runoff caused nearly twice the normal seasonal decline in deposits, and the loan/deposit ratio rose to 65.1 percent.

As far as the disciplinary powers of the Federal Reserve System are concerned, throughout the Kennedy era the Fed steadily permitted the massive growth in bank credit that the New Economics prescribed. During the Johnson years and the Vietnam war period it pursued a highly erratic course; first permitting a huge monetary expansion then suddenly cutting back in 1966, then—at the first real indication that the inflationary expectations were being shaken out of the securities markets—easing up again. Now the Governors are talking about putting the lid on and keeping it on until the inflationary psychology is finally smothered. *If* they mean it—and I believe they do—the banks have nowhere left to turn to evade the pressure, except to the partial and wildly dangerous expedient of further increasing their Eurodollar liabilities. And I do not think the Fed will permit them to go much farther in that direction.[2]

**There are enormous liquid liabilities
in the United States monetary system
that are not recognized in theory, and
against which little or no liquid
reserves are maintained**

Checking account deposits are the most conspicuous example of financial claims that the owner has a legally enforceable right to withdraw upon demand, and therefore monetary theory concentrates upon them almost exclusively. In my view, this is a drastic and dangerous oversimplification. Commercial banks' time deposits, Savings bank deposits, and Savings and Loan shares are traditionally redeemed on demand; and the public has become so accustomed to this convenience that the reputation of any institution that was not able to honor these obligations at sight would be hope-

---

[2]I was wrong; and it was the outflow of these funds in 1971, when interest rates declined in the United States, that precipitated the run on the dollar.

lessly compromised. These institutions typically do not hold large amounts of liquid assets; but most of them do have access to a Federal Agency that presumably would draw on the United States Treasury and advance them the funds to meet a net deposit withdrawal.

There is an even more glaring oversight in the conventional description of the American monetary system. The life insurance companies are never considered as being subject to liquid claims. Nevertheless it is a fact that the holders of most ordinary life policies have an *absolute* right to borrow the cash reserves behind their policies—*on demand, with no obligation to repay the loan, and typically at a 5 percent interest rate.* I have never attempted to estimate the potential liability for the industry as a whole; but I have done so for individual companies, and I believe that the total would considerably exceed *$50 billion.*[3] The life insurance companies hold almost no liquid assets (except common stocks, which we used to think could readily be turned into cash—although at an indefinite price. Of this more anon.) Nor do they have any legal right whatsoever to draw upon any public agency. However, I am told that during the 1966 crunch one company did quietly ask the Federal Reserve Board what would happen if a run on policy loans developed and was assured— also very quietly—that the Fed would stand behind them. Indeed, it would have to. The insolvency of a large life insurance company would undoubtedly trigger a liquidity crisis of epic proportions.

The current level of interest rates threatens massive disintermediation

In normal times total bank deposits grow steadily and bankers can get away with an asset administration policy that maximizes income at the expense of liquidity. Similarly, the premium income of life insurance companies usually enor-

---

[3] Since I have returned to the life insurance industry I have discovered that a more accurate figure in 1969 would have been approximately $100 billion. At the end of 1978 it was about $150 billion.

mously exceeds the relatively small volume of policy loans, withdrawals of the reserves behind annuity contracts, and the like. But these are emphatically not normal times in the financial world. The current level of interest rates is already high enough to tempt the holders of liquid claims against financial institutions to withdraw them and invest the money themselves. It is hard to think of a safer and surer way to increase your income than to borrow on your life insurance at 5 percent, or withdraw your savings deposits that are probably earning no more than 5½ percent and buy the Triple A-rated New York Telephone 7½'s of 2009 that came to market Tuesday at 101.6 to yield 7.38 percent to maturity. There are still plenty of them available—indeed, if anyone feels like doing this I would suggest that you wait until Morgan Stanley gives up and breaks the offering price.

A net contraction of liquid liabilities means a drop in national purchasing power

We have discussed the process by which an expansion of the monetary system's liquid liabilities increases purchasing power. The process works in reverse too—a runoff of liquid liabilities drains financial institutions of lendable funds and eventually forces the calling in of demand loans. When market rates are as high as they are at present, there is very little that the institutions can do to protect themselves. Since the bulk of their assets is invested at lower returns they cannot raise their earnings to cover a higher rate on their deposits any faster than their existing investments mature and the money can be rolled over into higher yielding instruments. Indeed, the life insurance companies aren't even helped by higher earnings. The policy loan rate was set when the policy was written and cannot be changed unilaterally.

We are certain to see a fair amount of disintermediation in 1969. The important question is—how much? Anyone who blithely assumes that interest rates can stay at current levels or go higher without a severe economic impact should contemplate the $200 billion of commercial bank time deposits, the $65 billion of savings bank deposits, the $131 billion of savings and loan certificates and the (estimated) $50+ billion of liquid claims against life insurance companies—all of which are earning, or available at, rates well below the going market price of money. The net withdrawal of even an infinitesimal fraction of these funds would produce a catastrophic shrinkage of national purchasing power. But that is not all.

And may cause a liquidity panic

Since the financial institutions hold only a very small volume of liquid assets against their potential liquid liabilities, a net shrinkage can easily get out of hand. Once a rumor starts that an institution is having trouble meeting its obligations, even the man who was happy to leave his money there suddenly wants it out very badly. That is how runs start. And once a few institutions are forced to suspend payments, virtually all become suspect. It is clear that the financial institutions could not satisfy any large net claims without calling on the Federal Reserve System and the other Agencies that have been established as lenders of last resort. If international conditions permitted, these bodies would lend freely in a pinch—that is what they're there for—but there is a fly in the ointment.

Our liquid international liabilities are a potential source of trouble

The external position of the United States is also shaky, from a liquidity point of view. Our total foreign assets enormously exceed our liabilities, but our current position is not so hot. Our liquid liabilities total more than $35 billion, against which we have about $16 billion in liquid assets. As long as this condition exists, the Authorities would be reluctant to print money wholesale to meet a domestic pinch.[4] Indeed,

---

[4]Events in 1971, and several incidents thereafter, proved that I was also wrong about this. In 1978 the Fed made credit readily available, admittedly at a high nominal rate of interest, while the external value of the dollar was collapsing.

there is a fair chance that a domestic liquidity crisis might be touched off by net foreign withdrawals.

So is the paperwork mess in Wall Street

Another potential trouble spot is the several billion dollars' worth of transactions on the stock exchanges that have not been settled because the bookkeeping is scrambled. It has forced the rest of the country to lend the Wall Street community a billion dollars or so involuntarily, and for an indefinite period. This situation is viable only as long as everybody remains confident that for every debit there *must* be a credit somewhere, and that the mess can eventually be unscrambled. If that confidence should disappear, a run on the brokerage houses and mutual funds would become not only possible but very probable. And if the life insurance companies are somewhat exposed because there is no lender of last resort who is obligated to back them up, the brokers and mutual funds are all alone in a cold, cruel world.

We probably cannot disinflate without deflationary crises

The fundamental market forces turned disinflationary a decade ago when the pressures of postwar hyperliquidity, domestic demands piled up during the Depression and war years, and net foreign demand all abated. The economy lapsed into noninflationary "normalcy" for a few years; but then, by a conscious, democratic decision we voted for a deliberate policy of inflationary restimulation. Now political and psychological forces have turned negative too, so that further deliberate inflation will only worsen the social tensions and conflicts that plague our nation. We must stop now, or risk the collapse of our organized and productive society. Our national political leaders and monetary authorities realize this—instinctively if not consciously—and we will stop. The shock, however, will be severe. In the long run it will be healthy, but in 1969 and 1970 several of the problems that we have discussed are virtually certain to become crises as the money flow stops and the Government develops a more modest view of its effective powers and responsibilities. In the securities markets, the shock will be traumatic.

THE OUTLOOK FOR THE SECURITIES MARKETS

Barring a unilateral withdrawal from Vietnam, I expect all securities markets to remain under pressure in the short run. However, the prime quality long bond market should begin to recover a bit from the present crisis level as the Federal Government repays debt on balance, municipal flotations slacken off under the double impact of statutory interest rate ceilings and the emerging taxpayers' rebellion, business inventory accumulation slackens, and it becomes clear that we are not going to have a runaway capital spending spree. If the Fed has the guts to stick to its guns as the economy softens the rally will be gradual; but the first step will have been taken toward restoring an effective and moderate-cost capital market that is essential to continued prosperity in the United States.

The medium-to-low quality bond market is so hopelessly glutted that it will take a good deal longer to recover. If the uncompromising monetary confrontation that I envision does indeed take place, there will be some defaults on lower grade corporate and municipal obligations; and we may see the emergence of a larger than normal yield premium for risk rather than the historically small one that now obtains.

The stock market will undoubtedly rally from time to time on rumors of peace or other cheerful tidings; but to me the fundamental direction looks to be clearly down.

Index